MEXICAN
COOKING

INTERNATIONAL GOURMET

MEXICAN COOKING

Carolyn Dehnel

WARD LOCK LIMITED · LONDON

First published in Great Britain in 1986 by
Ward Lock Limited, 8 Clifford Street,
London W1X 1RB, an Egmont Company.

Designed by Melissa Orrom.
Text filmset in Garamond Original by
M & R Computerised Typesetting Ltd.,
Grimsby.

Printed and bound in Portugal by Resopal.

British Library Cataloguing in Publication Data

Dehnel, Carolyn
Mexican cooking.
1. Cookery, Mexican
I. Title
641.5972 TX716.M4

ISBN 0-7063-6464-3

CONTENTS

Acknowledgements

Inside photography by David Burch

Home Economist – Lorna Rhodes

Line drawings by Lorraine Harrison

The publisher would like to thank the following for kindly loaning equipment for photography:
The Bramley Hedge Shop
Mexiclore

Notes

It is important to follow **either** the metric **or** the imperial measures when using the recipes in this book. Do not use a combination of measures.

All recipes serve four people, unless otherwise specified.

INTRODUCTION

Food in modern Mexico is as lively and colourful as its people, as dramatic as its history. It has the fierceness of its bullfighters, the subtlety of its silver filigree jewellery, the appeal of its colonial and modern architecture. Furthermore, it is high in fibre and protein, with a bias towards low-cholesterol fish and poultry.

Mexico's culinary tradition certainly pre-dates 1521 and the conquest of the Aztecs by Hernan Cortés. The Indians had a farming tradition rivalled in antiquity only by that of the Middle East, and their basic diet included corn (maize), tomatoes, avocado pears, a large variety of squashes, half a hundred different beans, plus a quantity of chillies unknown in the Old World. There was no sugar. The only sweetener was honey from the stingless bees of Yucatan, and this was reserved for the Indian nobility of Montezuma's Aztec kingdom.

Cortés and his Conquistadores found rooms of treasure in the Aztec capital of Tenochtitlan (today's Mexico City). The 'treasure' was *cacao* (cocoa) beans, which were the only currency in existence, being rarer than gold or silver, and less easy to obtain.

The Conquistadores very quickly introduced foods from the Old World. Wheat, goats, rice and citrus trees all became an integral part of the Indian farming economy.

Mexico remained a colonial outpost of Spain until the revolution, inspired by France and the United States, of 1821. However, its independence did not last long, for in 1862 the French invaded. They set up as Emperor the ill-fated Austrian, Maximilian, who ruled until 1867, when his defeat and execution by Mexican forces ended the French occupation.

The French court's chefs introduced a number of cooking methods and foods which were adopted by Mexican chefs. One example is the crème caramel on page 72. Maximilian became fond of Mexican chocolate, and served it as an after-dinner drink in preference to coffee.

One of the great lasting influences of the Spanish conquest of Mexico was the introduction of Christianity to the native population. The Indians accepted Christianity while keeping many of their own ways, and the result, even today, is an interesting mix of the pagan and the Christian. This is especially evident in the festivals that are so much a part of Mexican life.

All Saints Day and All Souls Day, November 1 and November 2, are celebrated with exuberance throughout Mexico. Breads, sweets and toys are sold, all in the shapes of bones, skulls and skeletons. One of the traditional breads is *Pan de Muerto* (page 78), which has a representation of the soul's bones and knuckles on the top. Special foods and drinks are prepared for the dead, and left in the cemeteries to be eaten by the souls. Morbid as it may sound, this is all taken lightly, and the two days of celebration are more like a huge picnic.

The greatest religious festival is Christmas. The celebrations begin on December 16 and last until Epiphany, January 6. On Christmas Day there is a feast of turkey, usually *Mole Poblano con Pollo* (page 45), with *Ensalada de Nochebuena* (page 66), and sweets and all the trimmings of a Mexican meal.

In Oaxaca, December 23 is celebrated as *Noche de Rábanos* (Radish Night). Large red radishes are in season, and they are cut into flowers and fantastic shapes, and left in cold water overnight. On the 23rd, houses, gardens, public buildings and restaurants are decorated with the radishes. That night, all over the city, *Buñuelos* (page 76) are sold on cracked and irregular Oaxaca pottery, which the vendor has been saving all year. Part of the fun is to eat the *Buñuelos* and then crash the plate to the ground, so that by Christmas Eve the plazas are filled with piles of broken pottery.

On Epiphany there is a celebration with family and friends. Special foods are prepared, including *Rosca de Reyes* (page 80), a ring of bread with a difference. There are three items hidden in the dough: a ring, a coin and a *niño* (a tiny china doll) or a bean. The recipient of the ring knows that there will be a wedding in his family that year, the recipient of the coin knows that he will have especially good luck, and the recipient of the *niño* or bean has to give a party for all present on February 2, which is Friendship Day.

There are two major patriotic holidays. The first is *El Cinco de Mayo*, (May 5), which celebrates the victory over the French at Puebla in 1862. The second, and more important, is *El Dieciséis de Septiembre* (September 16), the Mexican Independence Day.

Food served at these times takes on the colours of the Mexican flag: green, white and red. In September the favourite is *Chiles en Nogada* (page 38), which is supposed to have been invented in Puebla, in 1821, to celebrate the signing of the Constitution by Augustin Iturbide. Another popular dish is *Ensalada de Bandera Mexicana* (page 66).

As well as the national celebrations, there are the more local *fiesta*. Regardless of size, they all reflect the warmth and friendliness of the Mexican people, and their intense pride in their beautiful country and their history.

Ingredients

Mexican cooks prefer fresh ingredients. Markets in every village are piled high with the freshest and most colourful fruits, vegetables and an infinite variety of chillies, squash and tomatoes.

Pork lard is the favourite fat for cooking, but vegetable oils, especially corn oil, can easily be substituted with no loss of flavour. Butter is almost never used.

Sauces depend upon seeds and nuts, or reduction, for their thickness.

All the foods listed as basic ingredients should be available either in supermarkets, health food shops, or ethnic shops – West Indian, Chinese, Greek, Indian, Italian. Any which are not readily available have been indicated, and substitutes suggested.

AVOCADO PEARS (Aguacate) If possible, search out the black, knobbly skinned types, which have more flavour and are less watery than the green-skinned ones. If you rub an avocado pear with lime or lemon juice after cutting it, it will go dark more slowly. When mashing the fruit, as for *Guacamole* (page 20), use a plastic or silver fork, mix with lime or lemon juice, and pop the stone into the finished product. If possible, slice avocado pears just before serving.

BEANS (Frijoles) Pink beans (pintos or borlottis), red kidney or black beans are best. Use pintos or borlottis for *Frijoles de la Olla* (page 17). They are available from Italian delicatessens. Black beans are more difficult to find, but worth the effort. Canned beans can be substituted. **Important** All dried beans must be soaked for at least 5 hours or overnight, and the soaking water then discarded. The beans should then be boiled briskly in fresh water for *at least* 10 minutes. They can then be cooked as applicable.

CHAYOTE (Chow Chow) This is a light green heart-shaped squash available in most West Indian food shops. It is cooked with the skin on, and then stuffed or served with a sauce. The seed is considered a delicacy, and often goes to the cook. It can also be used as an unusual garnish. If *chayote* is not available, kohlrabi can be substituted.

CHEESE (Queso) Substitutes for Mexican cheeses are any of the light coloured, slightly salty cheeses, such as Lancashire, Wensleydale or Cheshire. Cheddar can sometimes be used, especially in strong flavoured dishes.

CHILLIES In the absence of the 90 or so Mexican varieties, the Mexican cook must make do with the fresh chillies available, together with the canned varieties.

Canned green chillies are large and very mild. They can be eaten as a pickle, or used as a garnish. They can be wrapped around cheese, battered and fried as in *Chiles Rellenos de Queso* (page 30). Pickled *jalapeño* peppers in brine are very hot. However, the heat can be reduced by de-seeding. Only the very brave would eat a *jalapeño* as a pickle. Use in dishes where a strong flavour and heat are desired. The red and green capsicum peppers can also be used. These can be skinned, split and seeded, and used instead of canned green chillies.

Note The 'heat' of any dish is very much a matter of personal taste. Where recipes call for chilli powder, you may prefer to use only a small quantity at first, and gradually add more if necessary, according to taste. The same applies to chillies. You can also de-seed chillies before use, in order to reduce their heat.

CHORIZO This sausage is readily available from Spain and Italy in most delicatessens. It usually needs to be skinned before being used.

CORIANDER (Cilantro) This is the basic herb in the Mexican kitchen. There are times when parsley is an acceptable substitute, but at other times, such as in the preparation of *Guacamole* (page 20), only coriander will do. It is available in either Greek or Indian shops or in good supermarkets. Coriander is sometimes sold with a bit of root still attached. Cut off the remaining root, and put in water in the refrigerator. It should last up to a week if treated this way.

CORN/SWEETCORN (Maíz) This is the basic ingredient in the Mexican cuisine. The ancient Indians had corn, and only with the advent of the Spanish did the Indians cultivate wheat. Use fresh sweetcorn, if available. If not, use either frozen or canned.

COURGETTES (Calabacitas) The courgette is one of the many squashes grown in Mexico. The gardener can gather the flowers and use them in soups, or flash-fry them as a garnish.

LIMES (Limas) This small green citrus fruit is more and more widely available in supermarkets. Lemon can be substituted, but at the expense of taste. There are dishes that require limes or nothing. *Cebiche* (page 54) needs the sweet tartness of the lime for its subtle taste; made with lemon it is nothing.

MASA HARINA This is corn flour which is especially prepared for the making of corn tortillas. There is no substitute. The corn is treated by being boiled in lime water for several hours. It is then drained and dried, the outer skin removed and the kernels ground into cornmeal. Do not confuse *masa harina* with yellow cornmeal or polenta. Look for *masa harina* in good delicatessens or health food shops.

NUTS (Nueces) Pecans are the most widely used. They are available in health food shops. Walnuts can be substituted, but with a sacrifice in taste. Green walnuts are required for *Chiles en Nogada* (page 38), though the ripe ones can be used. Almonds and peanuts are also used, either as garnishes or to thicken sauces.

POMEGRANATES The seeds are used as garnishes in both sweet and savoury dishes. They give a delightful crunch to dishes that are soft in texture, such as *Ensalada de Bandera Mexicana* (page 66). To get at the seeds, cut the fruit into quarters and scoop out the seeds with a spoon. Leave the bits of white pith that tie the seed to the skin.

SEEDS Sesame seeds, *pepitas* (pumpkin seeds) and pine nuts are all used as garnishes, and to thicken sauces. All are available either in health food shops, Italian delicatessens, or in the spice section of a supermarket. Pumpkin seeds can be roasted and flavoured to use like peanuts as an accompaniment to drinks (see *Pepitas* on page 90).

TOMATILLAS A green, tomato-like vegetable that is best fresh, but can sometimes be found in a can. It is a relative of the Cape gooseberry and looks very much like a Chinese lantern, with its husk that is removed before use. Green tomatoes can be used to give the same colour, but the flavour can never be duplicated with a substitute.

TOMATOES (Tomates) Use the large 'beef' tomatoes, which are similar to Mexican tomatoes, wherever possible. Salad tomatoes are a very poor second choice. There are recipes where canned tomatoes can be easily substituted with success, especially in sauces. When using canned tomatoes, do be careful to reduce the liquid.

TORTILLAS There are *tortillas de maíz* (corn tortillas) and *tortillas de harina* (flour tortillas). Corn tortillas require *masa harina* (see above), and the flour tortillas can be made with plain white flour. The flour tortilla is to be found mostly across Northern Mexico in the states of Sonora, Nueva Leon, Chihuahua, Coahuila and Tamaulipas. Canned tortillas are to be avoided.

VANILLA Vanilla comes from the stamen of an orchid, and is produced at Paplitan. It was introduced to the Spanish by the Aztecs. It is a good idea to keep a jar of vanilla sugar in the cupboard. Simply fill a jar with caster sugar and push in a couple of vanilla pods. Top up the sugar as needed. Vanilla pods can be boiled up in milk to infuse the flavour. Remove from the milk, wash with clean water, allow to dry and use again.

VINEGAR Use cider, white wine or distilled malt vinegar.

BASICS

The recipes in this chapter are the basics which one will use time and again in Mexican cooking. Many are foods which appear every day on the Mexican table, like tortillas, *tamales, frijoles* (beans) and the various *salsas* (sauces). Master these basic foods, and you will be well on the way to mastering the cuisine of Mexico.

Tortillas are basic bread. They appear at every meal from breakfast to late-night supper, and are used to roll meat in, to scoop, and as a bowl. You may not be able to pat a tortilla out between the palms of your hands as the village women do, but you will quickly become adept at pressing it out on a work surface, using the bottom of a small frying pan.

The *tamale*, wrapped and steamed in a corn husk *(hoja)* or banana leaf, dates from pre-Conquest Mexico. *Tamales* wrapped in foil taste just as good, even if they look less authentic. *Guacamole* is another basic food known from pre-Conquest times.

Many of these recipes freeze well, especially the *salsas*, with the exception of *Salsa Roja* (page 21), and tortillas, both corn and wheat. Freeze the *salsas* in serving-sized portions, in plastic containers with tight-fitting lids. Interleave the tortillas with pieces of greaseproof paper, and freeze in plastic bags. Both *salsas* and tortillas will keep in the freezer for up to six months.

Tortillas de Maíz
Corn Tortillas

Makes eighteen 7.5cm/3 inch tortillas or nine 15cm/6 inch tortillas

---

100ml/4 fl oz warm water
150g/5 oz masa harina
a pinch of salt

In a medium sized mixing bowl, work the water into the *masa harina* with your fingers until you have a firm but pliable dough. Cover with a tea-towel, then leave to rest for 20 minutes.

Have ready two squares of clingfilm. Divide the dough into either 9 or 18 balls. Place a ball of dough on one piece of clingfilm, and cover with the second piece. Press the dough with the palm of the hand until the dough is in a circle. With the bottom of a small frying pan or a tortilla press, press the dough into a circle of the desired diameter. Remove the piece of clingfilm carefully. Stack the tortillas with a piece of greaseproof paper between each. If the outer edge of the tortilla is ragged, the dough is too dry. Work a teaspoon of warm water into the dough. If the dough is too sticky, the clingfilm will not come away easily. Work a teaspoon of *masa harina* into the dough.

To bake, heat a griddle or heavy frying pan, and cook the dough on each side until lightly spotted with brown. Turn only once. Stack on a plate, and cover with a tea-towel. The tortillas will soften as they stand.

Use as required.

Corn and *Flour (page 16) Tortillas*

Tortillas de Harina
Flour Tortillas

Makes 12

275g/10 oz plain white flour
2 × 5ml spoons/2 teaspoons salt
100g/4 oz lard, cut into small pieces
100ml/4 fl oz warm water

Combine the flour and salt in a large bowl. Work in the lard, then gradually add the water, until you have a pliable dough. Knead for 5 minutes. Divide into 12 balls, and cover with a damp tea-towel. Roll each ball into a circle of approximately 25cm/10 inches on a floured work surface. The dough should be very thin.

To bake, heat a griddle or a large, heavy frying pan, and cook each tortilla, turning once. (Count to 40 as you cook each side.) Stack the cooked tortillas with a piece of greaseproof paper between each, and cover with a tea-towel. Use as required.

Totopos
Corn Crisps

corn oil for frying
10 Tortillas de Maíz *(page 14), each cut into 8 triangular wedges*
salt

Heat a pan of oil until a 2.5cm/1 inch cube of bread will brown in 1 minute. Fry the tortilla pieces until brown and crisp. This will take about 4 minutes. Do not overbrown. Remove from the oil and drain on kitchen paper. Sprinkle with salt. Do not overcrowd the pan when frying the *totopos.*

Note *Totopos* make a good snack on their own with drinks, or as a dipper.

Frijoles de la Olla
Basic Beans

275g/10 oz dried pinto or *borlotti beans*
1 clove of garlic
½ medium onion, chopped
2 × 5ml spoons/2 teaspoons chilli powder
2 × 5ml spoons/2 teaspoons salt

Cover the beans with water and soak overnight or for at least 5 hours. Drain off the soaking water, then rinse. Put the beans in a large pan and cover with fresh water. Bring to a boil and boil briskly for 15 minutes. Drain off the water and cover the beans with fresh water, or stock left from cooking beef or pork. Add the garlic, onion and chilli powder. Cook uncovered, for about 1 hour, until soft.

When the beans are cooked, add the salt. Check the seasoning. If you have used plain water, you may need more salt. Remove the garlic before serving. Use for *Frijoles con Chorizo* (page 40), *Frijoles Refritos* (page 64) or as an accompaniment to any Mexican meal.

Picadillo
Spiced Minced Beef Sauce

25g/1 oz lard
1 medium onion, chopped
675g/1½ lb minced beef
400g/14 oz canned tomatoes, undrained
175g/6 oz concentrated tomato purée
75g/3 oz raisins
2 × 15ml spoons/2 tablespoons red wine vinegar
1–6 × 5ml spoons/1–6 teaspoons chilli powder
1 × 5ml spoon/1 teaspoon ground cinnamon
1 × 5ml spoon/1 teaspoon ground cumin
1 × 5ml spoon/1 teaspoon sugar
a pinch of ground cloves
1–3 jalapeño *peppers* or *Kenya chillies, deseeded and finely chopped*

Melt the lard in a large pan and fry the onions for 5 minutes. Increase the heat, then add the minced beef and brown well. Add all the remaining ingredients, except the peppers, and simmer uncovered for 1½ hours. Add the chopped peppers.

Use in *Tamales* (page 18), *Tacos* (page 37), *Burritos* (page 34) and in *Chiles en Nogada* (page 38).

Tamales

Basic Tamales

Makes 12

---

12 dried corn husks or *12 pieces of foil, 15cm × 20cm/6 inches × 8 inches*
200g/7 oz lard
450g/1 lb masa harina
1 × 5ml spoon/1 teaspoon baking powder
1 × 5ml spoon/1 teaspoon salt
450ml/¾ pint warm water or *stock*
1 recipe filling, see Picadillo *(page 17)*, Tamales de Puerco *(page 38)*, Tamales de Pollo *(page 43)*

Prepare the dried corn husks by covering them with warm water and leaving to soak overnight.

In a large bowl beat the lard until the consistency of light cream. In a separate bowl mix the *masa harina*, baking powder and salt together. Gradually add the dry mixture to the beaten lard, alternately with the warm water. The dough should now be firm, but pliable. You may chill the dough at this point to use later.

Drain the corn husks, if using, and dry between two tea-towels. Spread the husks or pieces of foil on a work surface. Divide the dough among the husks/foil rectangles. Spread the dough into a rectangular form, leaving a 2.5cm/1 inch strip down one long side. Spoon 2 × 15ml spoons/2 tablespoons of filling down the centre of the dough. Fold over the long side of the husks/foil, then fold the narrow half over to make a packet open at one end.

As you make each *tamale*, stand it upright in a steamer or on a rack over water in a large pot. When you have filled the steamer with the *tamales*, cover with a damp tea-towel. Put the lid on the pot. Steam for 1½–2 hours. Check occasionally to ensure that the water has not boiled away.

Transfer to a platter and serve with a bowl of *salsa* (pages 21–22).

Chicken (page 43) and *Pork (page 38) Tamales* accompanied by *Salsa de Tomate (page 22)*

Guacamole

2 avocado pears
2 medium tomatoes, skinned and finely chopped
10 spring onions, chopped
1–2 jalapeño *peppers* or *Kenya chillies, de-seeded and finely chopped*
2 × 15ml spoons/2 tablespoons fresh lime or *lemon juice*
1 × 15ml spoon/1 tablespoon fresh coriander, chopped
salt and pepper

Mash the avocado pear in a medium bowl. It should have small bits of flesh still visible. Add the tomatoes, onions, *jalapeño* peppers, lime or lemon juice, coriander, salt and pepper. Check for seasoning.

Note This salad is best made just before serving.

Mantequilla de Pobre
Butter of the Poor

1 avocado pear
2 medium tomatoes, skinned and chopped
1 × 15ml spoon/1 tablespoon corn oil
2 × 15ml spoons/2 tablespoons fresh lime or *lemon juice*
1 × 2.5ml spoon/½ teaspoon salt

Mash the avocado pear until very smooth or process in a blender or food processor. Add the tomatoes, corn oil, lime or lemon juice and salt. Continue to mash and beat until the consistency of very soft butter.
Serve as an accompaniment to *Carne Asada* (page 36), or use as a spread for sandwiches as a substitute for butter.

Vinagreta
Vinaigrette

75ml/3 fl oz corn oil
25ml/1 fl oz lemon juice
1 clove of garlic, crushed
1 × 5ml spoon/1 teaspoon salt
1 × 5ml spoon/1 teaspoon mustard powder
freshly ground black pepper

Combine all the ingredients in a glass jar. Cover with the lid and shake vigorously.
Use as required.

Salsa Roja
Red Sauce

225g/8 oz juicy tomatoes, skinned and chopped
1 jalapeño *pepper* or *Kenya chilli, de-seeded and finely chopped*
8 sprigs of coriander, chopped
12 spring onions, roughly chopped
¾ × 5ml spoon/¾ teaspoon salt
2 × 5ml spoons/2 teaspoons fresh lime or *lemon juice*
1 × 5ml spoon/1 teaspoon olive oil
1 clove of garlic, crushed

Combine all the ingredients in a small bowl. Cover and chill for at least 2 hours. This sauce improves with keeping. It will keep in the refrigerator for up to a week.
Use as required.

Note This sauce is not suitable for freezing.

Salsa Verde
Green Sauce

---

1 × 15ml spoon/1 tablespoon corn oil
1 medium onion, chopped
450g/1 lb green tomatoes or *tomatillos, if available, skinned and chopped*
2 × 15ml spoons/2 tablespoons fresh coriander, chopped
1–2 jalapeño *peppers* or *Kenya chillies, chopped*
100ml/4 fl oz chicken stock or *1 stock cube dissolved in 100ml/4 fl oz water*
salt and pepper

Heat the oil in a heavy based pan. Add the chopped onion and cook until golden. Add the chopped tomatoes and cook uncovered for 10 minutes. Either mash the mixture with a potato masher, or process in an electric blender. Add the coriander, *jalapeño* pepper and chicken stock. Cover and simmer gently for 30 minutes. Check occasionally to ensure that the mixture does not catch and burn. Season to taste.
Use as required.

Note This sauce is best made a day ahead.

Salsa de Tomate
Tomato Sauce

1 × 15ml spoon/1 tablespoon corn oil
¼ medium onion, finely chopped
1 clove of garlic, crushed
225g/8 oz canned tomatoes
1 × 5ml spoon/1 teaspoon oregano
1 jalapeño *pepper* or *Kenya chilli, de-seeded and chopped (optional)*
salt and pepper

Heat the oil in a heavy based pan. Cook the onion and garlic until the onion is lightly brown, approximately 5 minutes. Add the tomatoes. Stir, cutting the tomatoes into small pieces. Add the remaining ingredients. Simmer uncovered for 15 minutes.
Use as required.

Note You can make the sauce hotter by not de-seeding the *jalapeño* or by adding another de-seeded *jalapeño* pepper.

Salsa Picante
Hot Sauce

1 × 15ml spoon/1 tablespoon corn oil
½ large onion
1 clove of garlic, crushed
400g/14 oz canned tomatoes
2 × 15ml spoons/2 tablespoons concentrated tomato purée
1 jalapeño *pepper* or *Kenya chilli, de-seeded*
1 × 15ml spoon/1 tablespoon liquid from the jalapeño
salt and pepper

Heat the oil in a heavy based pan. Cook the onion and garlic until softened. Add the tomatoes and tomato purée. Simmer uncovered for 10 minutes. Remove from the heat, and add the *jalapeño* pepper and liquid. Process in an electric blender until smooth, or push the pulp through a sieve. Return to the heat and cook, uncovered, for a further 15 minutes. Season to taste.
Use as required.

SOUPS & STARTERS

There is only one way to begin a meal in Mexico, and that is with soup. There are two types of soup. *Sopa aguada* (wet soups) are covered in this chapter – they are the stock or water based soups with which we are familiar. *Sopa seca* (dry soups) are served after the *sopa aguada*, and look more like bowls of rice or pasta to the non-Mexican eye. Any of the rice recipes on pages 68–69 would qualify as a *sopa seca*.

Starter soups range from the hearty, such as *Cocido* (page 25), which would make a substantial lunch course on a cold day, to the very cooling *Sopa de Aguacate* (page 26). Mexican soups often tend to be bland, and are given a 'sting' by the addition of *salsa* or a squeeze of lime at the table.

Before the soup, *antojitos* (little savouries) are served with drinks (see pages 88–93 for recipes).

The other recipes in this chapter are also suitable as starters, although in Mexico they would normally be eaten as part of a light snack or supper. Many could equally well form a main course. There are several dishes in other chapters which also make good starters, such as *Cebiche* (page 54).

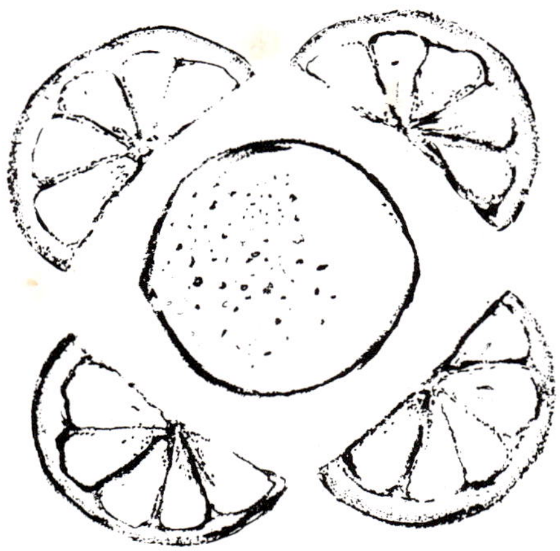

Sopa de Frijoles Negros
Black Bean Soup

225g/8 oz black beans
1 meaty ham or *pork bone*
2 onions, coarsely chopped
1 clove of garlic, chopped
2 large tomatoes, skinned and chopped
1 jalapeño *pepper* or *Kenya chilli, de-seeded and chopped*
salt and pepper
GARNISH:
fresh coriander, chopped

Cover the beans with water and soak overnight. Drain off the soaking water, and rinse.

In a large pan, cover the beans with water, and bring to a boil. Boil briskly, uncovered, for 15 minutes. Drain off the water and cover with fresh water. Add the ham or pork bone. Simmer for 1 hour or until the beans are soft. Remove the pork bone. Strip any meat from the bone and add to the beans. Add the remaining ingredients and simmer, uncovered, for a further 30 minutes. The soup should be thick. Season to taste. Serve garnished with chopped fresh coriander.

Sopa de Elote
Corn Soup

1 × 15ml spoon/1 tablespoon corn oil
1 medium onion, finely chopped
1 Kenya chilli, de-seeded and chopped
½ green pepper, chopped
½ red pepper, chopped
600ml/1 pint chicken stock
300ml/½ pint creamy milk
350g/12 oz sweetcorn
2 tomatoes, skinned, de-seeded and chopped
2 × 5ml spoons/2 teaspoons salt
freshly ground white pepper
GARNISH:
fresh coriander, chopped

Heat the oil in a large pan. Cook the onion and chilli until the onion is just transparent. Do not brown. Add the red and green peppers, and coat with the oil. Allow to cook for just 1 minute. Add the chicken stock and milk, and bring to a boil. Reduce the heat immediately. Add the sweetcorn, tomatoes and salt. Simmer, uncovered for 30 minutes. Check the seasoning. Serve with chopped fresh coriander sprinkled on the top.

Sopa de Tortilla
Tortilla Soup

2 × 15ml spoons/2 tablespoons corn oil
½ medium onion, thinly sliced
3 canned green chillies, drained and chopped
1 litre/1¾ pints chicken stock
175g/6 oz cooked chicken
2 × 15ml spoons/2 tablespoons fresh lime juice
1 tomato, skinned, de-seeded and chopped
salt and pepper
GARNISH:
thin slices of lime
Totopos *(page 16)*

Heat the oil in a large pan, and cook the onion until transparent. Add the chillies, chicken stock, chicken, lime juice and tomato. Simmer covered for 30 minutes. Season to taste.

To serve, put 2 *Totopos* in the bottom of a soup plate. Pour the soup over and garnish with a slice of lime. Serve extra *Totopos* in a bowl.

Cocido
Beef Marrow Soup

1 large marrow bone
900g/2 lb braising steak, trimmed and cut into 5cm/2 inch cubes
1 small onion
salt and pepper
2 large carrots, cut into 5cm/2 inch slices
2 courgettes, cut into 5cm/2 inch slices
2 ears of sweetcorn, cut into quarters
1 large onion, chopped
1 potato, thickly sliced
GARNISH:
Arroz Rojo *(page 69)*
Salsa Roja *(page 21)*
wedges of lime

In a large pan, cover the marrow bone, braising steak and small onion with cold water. Bring to a boil and skim for 5 minutes. Reduce the heat and simmer uncovered for 1½ hours.

Strain off the stock and skim. Return the meat and the stock to the pan. Season to taste. Add the vegetables and simmer for 30 minutes. This soup is best made a day ahead.

Serve a portion of *Arroz Rojo* in a soup plate or bowl, then pour over the soup. Top with the *Salsa Roja*. Garnish with a wedge of fresh lime.

Sopa de Albóndigas
Meatball Soup

225g/8 oz minced beef
225g/8 oz minced pork
1 egg, beaten
1 × 5ml spoon/1 teaspoon dried oregano
½ medium onion, finely chopped
2 × 15ml spoons/2 tablespoons fresh coriander, chopped
1 × 5ml spoon/1 teaspoon salt
1 litre/1¾ pints beef stock
½ green pepper, roughly chopped
1 onion, thinly sliced
450g/1 lb tomatoes, skinned and chopped
2 carrots, thinly sliced
salt and pepper

First make the meatballs by mixing the beef and pork together well. Add the egg, oregano, onion, coriander and the teaspoon of salt, and mix. Divide into portions of 25g/1 oz each, and roll into meatballs.

Meanwhile, bring the stock to a gentle simmer in a large pot.

Drop the meatballs into the simmering broth. Bring back to a boil and skim off any foam. Cover and cook gently for 30 minutes. Add the pepper, onion, tomatoes and carrots and cook uncovered for a further 25 minutes or until the vegetables are cooked. Season to taste.

Sopa de Aguacate
Cold Avocado Soup

2 large avocado pears, well ripened
1 × 15ml spoon/1 tablespoon fresh lime juice
300ml/½ pint single cream
150ml/¼ pint milk
300ml/½ pint strained chicken stock
1 × 5ml spoon/1 teaspoon salt
freshly ground white pepper
GARNISH:
150ml/¼ pint soured cream
spring onions or *fresh coriander, chopped*

Mash the avocado pears with the lime juice until very smooth, or process in an electric blender or food processor. Beat in the cream and milk until well blended. Add the chicken stock, salt and pepper. Check the seasoning. Extra lime juice may be needed. Refrigerate until well chilled.

Serve in soup bowls with a spoon of soured cream, and a further garnish of spring onions or fresh coriander leaves.

Wet and Dry Soups
Arroz Mexicano (page 68), Meatball Soup and *Cold Avocado Soup*

Burritos de Frijoles Y Queso
Burritos with Beans and Cheese

8 cooked Tortillas de Harina *(page 16) (see* **Note***)*
Frijoles Refritos *(page 64)*
100g/4 oz Cheddar cheese, grated
300ml/½ pint soured cream
¼ head iceberg lettuce, shredded
225g/8 oz tomatoes, chopped

In the centre of each tortilla, layer *Frijoles Refritos*, cheese, soured cream, lettuce and tomatoes. Bring the four opposite sides to the centre so a square parcel is formed. Serve immediately, or the *burrito* will be soggy.

Note The tortillas should be hot but still soft.

Chalupas
Filled Boat-Shaped Tortillas

8 Tortillas de Maíz *(page 14)*
corn oil for frying
Frijoles Refritos *(page 64)*
¼ medium onion, chopped
Salsa Picante *(page 22)*
175g/6 oz Cheddar cheese, grated

GARNISH:
spring onions with tops, chopped
sprigs of fresh coriander
150ml/¼ pint soured cream
olives, stoned and chopped

Roll the tortillas out in an oval shape between two sheets of clingfilm, or press them out with the back of a small frying pan. Cook them by frying in a shallow pan of oil. Remove from the oil and drain on kitchen paper. Keep the tortillas soft by covering with a damp tea-towel.

When all the tortillas are cooked, and while they are still soft, pinch the side all around to make a boat-shaped tortilla. This can only be done while the tortillas are soft.

Fill each tortilla boat with *Frijoles Refritos*, chopped onion, *Salsa Picante* and cheese. Serve each tortilla boat with a garnish of spring onions, coriander, soured cream and olives.

Quesadilla de Queso
Cheese Quesadilla

4 large Tortillas de Harina *(page 16)*
225g/8 oz Cheddar cheese, grated
225g/8 oz tomatoes, skinned and chopped
8 spring onions, chopped
Salsa Picante *(page 22)*

GARNISH:
Guacamole *(page 20)*
lettuce, shredded
green olives, stoned and chopped

Layer one-quarter of the cheese, tomatoes and onions on one-half of each tortilla. Top with the *Salsa Picante*. Fold the unfilled half of the tortilla over. Bake in a moderate oven, 180°C/350°F/Gas 4, for 10–15 minutes or until the cheese is melted. Serve on plates with a garnish of *Guacamole*, lettuce and chopped olives.

Quesadilla con Ensalada
Quesadilla with Salad

8 Tortillas de Maíz *(page 14)*
225g/8 oz Cheddar cheese, grated
1 medium onion, thinly sliced
corn oil for frying
4 tomatoes, skinned and chopped
1 avocado pear, chopped
Salsa Verde *(page 21)*

Fill one-half of the tortilla with 25g/1 oz of cheese and a slice of onion. Fold the unfilled side over and seal by pressing the outer edges together. Shallow fry in oil. The *quesadilla* will take about 2 minutes on each side. Do not allow to burn.

Serve the *quesadilla* with a salad of the remaining onion, tomatoes and avocado pear. Serve the *Salsa Verde* separately.

Enchiladas de Queso
Cheese Enchiladas

8 Tortillas de Maíz *(page 14)*
corn oil for frying
Salsa Picante *(page 22)*
275g/10 oz Cheddar or *Wensleydale cheese, grated*
1 onion, finely chopped
300ml/½ pint soured cream (optional)
GARNISH:
avocado pear, sliced

Dip each tortilla into a pan of hot corn oil for 5 seconds, or until softened. Drain on kitchen paper and dip in the *Salsa Picante*.
Arrange on each softened tortilla, 25g/1 oz cheese, some chopped onion, and 1 × 15ml spoon/1 tablespoon of soured cream, if using. Roll the tortilla up tightly and place, seam down, in a medium baking dish. If the *enchiladas* come unrolled, place a knife across each end to keep them in place.
When all the tortillas are rolled into *enchiladas*, cover with the remaining *salsa*, cheese and onion. Bake in a moderate oven, 180°C/350°F/Gas 4, for 30 minutes. Garnish with the avocado pear. Serve the remaining soured cream separately, if used.

Chiles Rellenos de Queso
Chillies Stuffed with Cheese

8 canned green chillies, drained
225g/8 oz Wensleydale or *Lancashire cheese*
2 eggs, separated
50g/2 oz plain flour
corn oil for frying
Salsa de Tomate *(page 22)*

Select 8 whole chillies. Slice the cheese into strips the length of the chillies. Place one piece of cheese in each chilli, and wrap the chilli around. Use a toothpick to secure the chilli around the cheese, if necessary.
Beat the egg whites until stiff. In a separate bowl, beat the egg yolks well, and mix with the egg whites. Spread the flour on a plate, or on a piece of paper. Heat a pan of oil until a 2.5cm/1 inch cube of bread browns in 1 minute. Dip each chilli into the flour, then into the egg mixture. Fry until golden.
Serve 2 chillies per person, with a small bowl of *Salsa de Tomate* for dipping.

Cheese Enchiladas

Chiles Rellenos de Guacamole
Stuffed Chillies with Guacamole

¼ red pepper, finely chopped
Guacamole *(page 20)*
8 canned green chillies, drained
GARNISH:
4 large lettuce leaves
¼ medium onion, thinly sliced
1 avocado pear, thinly sliced lengthways
Vinagreta *(page 20)*

Mix the chopped red pepper into the *Guacamole*. Fill each of the chillies with one-eighth of the *Guacamole* mixture.

Arrange the lettuce on 4 plates. Put 2 stuffed chillies on each plate, and garnish with the sliced onion and avocado pear. Drizzle the *Vinagreta* over. Ensure that both the stuffed chillies and the salad are dressed with the *Vinagreta*.

Chiles Rellenos de Frijoles
Stuffed Chillies with Beans

½ recipe quantity Frijoles Refritos *(page 64)*
½ green pepper, finely chopped
8 canned green chillies, drained
GARNISH:
tomatoes, quartered
onion rings, thinly sliced

Mix the *Frijoles Refritos* with the green pepper, and fill each chilli with the bean mixture. Refrigerate and chill well.

Serve 2 stuffed chillies on each plate. Garnish with the tomatoes and onion rings.

Note *Totopos* (page 16) make a nice crunchy accompaniment to this starter.

MEAT, POULTRY & EGGS

Good meat and poultry have always been available in Mexico, even in pre-Conquest days. Cortés and his men were astounded to see Montezuma choose his meal from a range of 30 dishes prepared with meat. Chicken and pork are especially popular, and beef is of top quality. Regional specialities include roast sucking pig and barbecued kid *(cabrito)*.

In Yucatan, *cabrito* is cooked in a *pib* (a stone pit), as is *Pollo Pibil* (page 44). This is wrapped in a banana leaf in Yucatan, but it tastes almost the same wrapped in foil, and baked in an ordinary oven.

Mexico's most famous chicken dish, if not its national dish, is *Mole Poblano con Pollo* (page 45) or *con Pavo* (turkey). A *molé* is a mixture, and what a mixture *Mole Poblano* is! The name means *mole* in the style of Puebla, and tradition has it that the dish was first prepared by the nuns of the Convent of Santa Rosa in Puebla. They prepared a dinner to thank their benefactor, a bishop, who had authorized an extension to the convent, and in their excitement used almost every ingredient in the larder, including chocolate. *Mole Poblano* can have between 20 and 35 ingredients, depending on the recipe, but the dish is worthy of the time and effort required to prepare it. There is a short cut available in the form of *mole* paste or powder, but it can never produce the same results.

Tamales del Horno
Baked Tamales

1 × 15ml spoon/1 tablespoon butter
8 Tamales (page 18)
300ml/½ pint soured cream
Salsa de Tomate *(page 22)*
100g/4 oz Cheddar cheese, grated

Butter a medium ovenproof casserole. Cut the *tamales* into 2.5cm/1 inch slices and arrange on the bottom of the casserole. Pour the soured cream over, then the *Salsa de Tomate* and finish with the grated cheese. Bake in a moderate oven, 180°C/350°F/Gas 4, for 30 minutes.

Note This is a very good way to use up left-over *tamales*, and is also a convenient way to serve *tamales* at a party.

Burritos de Picadillo
Burritos with Beef

8 Tortillas de Harina *(page 16)*
½ recipe quantity Picadillo *(page 17)*
100g/4 oz Cheddar cheese, grated

GARNISH:
Guacamole *(page 20)*
iceberg lettuce, shredded
tomatoes, chopped

In the centre of each tortilla, spread one-eighth of the *Picadillo* and one-eighth of the cheese. Bring the four opposite sides to the centre, to form a square parcel. Arrange the *burritos* in a single layer in a shallow, ovenproof casserole and bake in a fairly hot oven, 200°C/400°F/Gas 6, for 15 minutes. The *burritos* will be crisp. Garnish with the *Guacamole*, shredded lettuce and tomato.

Burritos with Beef

Carne Asada
Roasted Meat

4 × 150g/4 × 5 oz sirloin steaks, well trimmed
MARINADE:
50ml/2 fl oz fresh lime juice
50ml/2 fl oz corn oil
a pinch of chilli powder
1 × 5ml spoon/1 teaspoon salt
1 × 2.5ml spoon/½ teaspoon pepper
GARNISH:
lime slices

Make the marinade first. Combine the lime juice, corn oil, chilli powder, salt and pepper in a large bowl or dish. Marinate the steaks for at least 2 hours. Drain the marinade from the steaks, and grill or dry fry. Garnish with the lime slices.

Serve with *Mantequilla de Pobre* (page 20).

Torta de Enchiladas
Enchilada Flan

9 Tortillas de Maíz *(page 14)*
225g/8 oz minced beef
1 medium onion, finely chopped
1 clove of garlic, crushed
1 × 5ml spoon/1 teaspoon ground cumin
1 × 15ml spoon/1 tablespoon chilli powder
1 × 5ml spoon/1 teaspoon salt
Salsa Picante *(page 22)*
225g/8 oz Cheddar cheese, grated
GARNISH:
green olives, stoned
1 green chilli, chopped
150ml/¼ pint soured cream (optional)

Cook the tortillas until crisp. Either fry in corn oil, or cook on both sides on a hot griddle or heavy based frying pan.

Fry the meat with the onion and garlic until it is well browned. Drain off most of the fat. Add the cumin, chilli powder and salt. Cook, uncovered, for a further 10 minutes.

In an ovenproof casserole, layer the tortillas, meat mixture, *Salsa Picante* and cheese. Finish with the cheese. Bake in a fairly hot oven, 190°C/375°F/Gas 5, for 30–40 minutes, until the cheese is well browned. Allow the flan to cool for 3–5 minutes. Cut into quarters and serve garnished with the olives, chilli and soured cream, if using.

Tacos de Picadillo
Beef Tacos

corn oil for frying
8 Tortillas de Maíz *(page 14)*
½ recipe quantity Picadillo *(page 17), warmed*
100g/4 oz Cheddar cheese, grated
Salsa Picante *(page 22), warmed*
¼ iceberg lettuce, shredded
225g/8 oz tomatoes, chopped

Make the *taco* shell first. Heat the oil 15cm/6 inches deep in a deep pan. Dip the tortilla into the hot oil. As it begins to cook, use a spatula to bring one-half up so that the tortilla is folded almost in half, but with a space of approximately 3.75cm/1½ inches between the two top edges. Cook for 3–4 minutes until crisp. This is the *taco* shell, which will be filled with the remaining ingredients. Drain the shells on kitchen paper. Keep warm in a very cool oven, 110°C/225°F/Gas ¼.

When all the shells are made, prepare the *tacos* by layering in the shell the *Picadillo*, cheese, *Salsa Picante*, lettuce and tomato.

Note The *tacos* are to be eaten with the fingers – not knives and forks.

Tamal
Tamale Pie

450g/1 lb minced beef
2 onions, chopped
1 × 5ml spoon/1 teaspoon chilli powder
a pinch of cayenne pepper
450g/1 lb tomatoes, skinned and chopped
salt
750ml/1¼ pints water
275g/10 oz cornmeal or *polenta*

Brown the meat in its own fat in a medium pan, breaking it up as it cooks. Add the onions, chilli powder, cayenne pepper, tomatoes and salt to taste. Mix well. Cover and cook for 1 hour.

Meanwhile, bring the water to a boil, and slowly add the cornmeal and 1 × 2.5ml spoon/½ teaspoon salt. Stir until very smooth. Reduce the heat and simmer for 30 minutes.

Spread half the cornmeal mixture in a 20cm/8 inch square dish. Spread the meat on top. Cover with the remaining cornmeal mixture. Bake in a moderate oven, 180°C/350°F/Gas 4, for 1 hour. The top will be a golden-brown.

Chiles en Nogada
Chillies in Nut Sauce

4 green peppers, skinned
½ recipe quantity Picadillo *(page 17) made with boneless pork*
SAUCE:
40g/1½ oz cream cheese
75g/3 oz green walnuts, ground
15g/½ oz caster sugar
25ml/1 fl oz brandy
75ml/3 fl oz creamy milk
GARNISH:
seeds from 1 pomegranate
shredded lettuce

Slit each pepper down one long side. Remove the seed and pith. Stuff with the *Picadillo*. Arrange each pepper on a bed of shredded lettuce. Meanwhile, prepare the sauce. Either process all the ingredients together in an electric blender until smooth, or allow the cheese to soften and cream in the walnuts. Add the sugar and brandy. Beat in the milk. The sauce will be thick. Top the meat stuffing in the pepper with the sauce. Scatter pomegranate seeds over the sauce.

Note The finished dish should be green, white and red—the colours of the Mexican flag.

Tamales de Puerco
Pork Tamales

1 × 15ml spoon/1 tablespoon corn oil
1 large onion, chopped
675g/1½ lb tomatoes, skinned and chopped
1 × 2.5ml spoon/½ teaspoon oregano
1 × 2.5ml spoon/½ teaspoon ground cumin
½ × 2.5ml spoon/¼ teaspoon garlic salt
1 × 15ml spoon/1 tablespoon malt vinegar
2 pickled jalapeño *peppers*
1 × 5ml spoon/1 teaspoon salt
450g/1 lb boneless pork shoulder, cooked and shredded
1 recipe quantity Tamale *dough (page 18)*

Heat the oil in a large pan. Cook the onion until browned. Add the tomatoes with the oregano, ground cumin and garlic salt. Cover, and cook for 10 minutes. Add the malt vinegar, *jalapeño* peppers and salt. Mix well. Add the pork, and combine well with the tomato mixture. Check the seasoning. Proceed as for *Tamales* (page 18).

Chillies in Nut Sauce

Pozole
Meat and Hominy Stew

2 × 15ml spoons/2 tablespoons corn oil
450g/1 lb boneless pork, cut into 5cm/2 inch cubes
½ chicken, jointed
1 large onion, chopped
2 cloves of garlic, crushed
450g/1 lb hominy or *sweetcorn*
1–9 × 5ml spoons/1–9 teaspoons chilli powder
2 × 5ml spoons/2 teaspoons salt
GARNISH:
Salsa Roja *(page 21)*
1 purple onion, chopped
1 bunch of radishes, sliced
fresh coriander, chopped
shredded lettuce
fresh lime wedges

Heat the oil in a large pan with a cover. Brown the cubes of pork in the oil, and remove to a plate. Next, brown the chicken pieces, and remove to the plate. Lastly, brown the onion and garlic. Return the pork and chicken to the pot. Cover with water. Bring to a boil. Skim off all scum which rises to the top. Cover, and cook gently until the meat is tender, about 1 hour. Add the hominy, chilli powder and salt. Cook for a further hour. Check the seasoning. More salt may be required.

Serve in large soup plates, with the garnishes passed separately.

Frijoles con Chorizo
Beans with Chorizo

100g/4 oz chorizo, *skin removed*
Frijoles de la Olla *(page 17), drained, garlic removed*
100g/4 oz Cheddar cheese, grated

Cook the *chorizo* in a shallow flameproof casserole for 10 minutes. Gradually add the *Frijoles*, mashing the mixture with a potato masher or the back of a spoon. When all the beans are incorporated into the *chorizo*, sprinkle the grated cheese on the top. Grill for 5 minutes.

Serve with *Totopos* (page 16).

Garbanzos Mexicanos
Mexican Chick Peas

225g/8 oz dried chick peas
1 × 15ml spoon/1 tablespoon lard
½ medium onion, chopped
300ml/½ pint Salsa Picante *(page 22)*
2 × 5ml spoons/2 teaspoons ground cumin
1–3 × 5ml spoons/1–3 teaspoons chilli powder
225g/8 oz chorizo, *in 2.5cm/1 inch slices*
1 red pepper, chopped
GARNISH:
fresh coriander, chopped

Soak the chick peas overnight in cold water. Drain, and discard the water. In a medium pot, cover the chick peas with fresh water, and bring to a boil. Boil briskly for 15 minutes. Drain again, and cover with fresh water or stock. Bring back to the boil, and simmer until the chick peas are tender. This will take approximately 1 hour.

Meanwhile, melt the lard in a large pan, and cook the onion until golden. Add the *salsa*, ground cumin, chilli powder, *chorizo* and red pepper. Bring to a boil, then simmer for 10 minutes.

Add the cooked chick peas, then cook, uncovered, until the mixture is thick and hot. Serve garnished with the chopped coriander.

Budín de Moctezuma
Mexican Casserole

Totopos *(page 16)*
450g/1 lb cooked chicken
600ml/1 pint soured cream
Salsa Verde *(page 21)*
225g/8 oz Wensleydale cheese, grated
GARNISH:
avocado pear, sliced

In a medium ovenproof casserole, layer the ingredients in the order given. Repeat the layers at least 3 times. Bake in a moderate oven, 180°C/350°F/Gas 4, for 30 minutes. Serve garnished with the slices of avocado pear.

Mancha Manteles
Tablecloth Stainer – Chicken and Pork

½ chicken, jointed
225g/8 oz pork, cut into 2.5cm/1 inch cubes
1 × 15ml spoon/1 tablespoon corn oil
1 medium onion, chopped
2 cloves of garlic, crushed
1–2 Kenya chillies, chopped
350g/12 oz tomatoes, chopped
25g/1 oz peanuts
1 bay leaf
1 × 5ml spoon/1 teaspoon ground cinnamon
1–3 × 5ml spoons/1–3 teaspoons chilli powder
3 whole cloves
1 × 15ml spoon/1 tablespoon sesame seeds
1 × 15ml spoon/1 tablespoon concentrated tomato purée
1 green pepper, chopped
1 plantain or *1 banana cut into 2.5cm/1 inch slices*
1 pear, sliced
1 cooking apple, sliced

Put the chicken and pork in a large pan, and cover with water. Simmer for 1 hour. Drain and reserve the stock.

Heat the oil in a large pan. Cook the onion, garlic and chillies until lightly browned. Add the tomatoes and continue to cook, uncovered, for a further 5 minutes. Add the peanuts, bay leaf, cinnamon, chilli powder, whole cloves and sesame seeds. Simmer uncovered, for 10 minutes. Process in an electric blender until smooth, or remove the cloves and push through a sieve or food mill. Return to the pan. Add the tomato purée, green pepper and the stock. If the sauce is too thin, simmer until thickened. Add the chicken, pork, plantain, pear and apple. Simmer for 10 minutes. If a plantain is not available, use a banana, but only add it in the last 5 minutes, otherwise it will disintegrate.

Serve with *Arroz Blanco* (page 68).

Arroz con Pollo
Rice with Chicken

1 × 15ml spoon/1 tablespoon corn oil
1 medium onion, cut in half and sliced
1 clove of garlic, crushed
175g/6 oz long grain white rice
475ml/16 fl oz chicken stock
1 × 5ml spoon/1 teaspoon salt
2 × 15ml spoons/2 tablespoons fresh lime juice
225g/8 oz canned tomatoes
550g/1¼ lb cooked chicken pieces
12 green olives, stoned
½ red pepper, sliced into strips
1 green chilli, sliced into strips
GARNISH:
lime quarters

Heat the oil in a flameproof casserole. Cook the onion and garlic until lightly browned. Add the rice. Continue to cook until the rice is browned. Add the chicken stock, salt, lime juice and tomatoes, and bring to a boil. Remove from the heat. Place the pieces of chicken over the rice. Cover and cook in a moderate oven, 180°C/350°F/Gas 4, for 20 minutes. Arrange the olives, slices of pepper and chilli on top of the chicken, cover, and cook for a further 10 minutes. Check to ensure that all the liquid has been absorbed. If it has not, cook uncovered for a further 5 minutes. Serve garnished with quarters of fresh lime.

Tamales de Pollo
Chicken Tamales

1 × 15ml spoon/1 tablespoon corn oil
1 medium onion, finely chopped
6 cloves of garlic, crushed
675g/1½ lb tomatoes, skinned and chopped
2 × 15ml spoons/2 tablespoons concentrated tomato purée
4 canned green chillies, drained and chopped
1 × 5ml spoon/1 teaspoon salt
white pepper
a pinch of sugar
450g/1 lb cooked chicken, shredded
1 recipe quantity Tamale *dough (page 18), made with chicken stock*

Heat the oil in a large pan. Cook the onion and garlic until soft. Add the tomatoes and tomato purée. Stir until the liquid in the tomatoes begins to run. Cook, uncovered, for a further 5 minutes. Add the chillies, salt, pepper and sugar. Cook, uncovered, for 3–5 minutes. The mixture should be just slightly liquid. Check the seasoning. Add the chicken, and mix well. Proceed as for *Tamales* (page 18).

Enchiladas de Pollo
Chicken Enchiladas

8 Tortillas de Maíz *(page 14)*
corn oil for frying
Salsa Picante *(page 22)*
275g/10 oz Cheddar or *Wensleydale cheese, grated*
225g/8 oz cooked chicken
1 onion, finely chopped
1 canned green chilli, drained and sliced lengthways into 8 slices
300ml/½ pint soured cream

Dip each tortilla into a pan of hot oil for 5 seconds, or until softened. Drain on kitchen paper, and dip in the *Salsa Picante*.

Arrange on each softened tortilla, 25g/1 oz of cheese, 25g/1 oz of chicken, chopped onion, one slice of green chilli, 1 × 15ml spoon/1 tablespoon *Salsa Picante* and 1 × 15ml spoon/1 tablespoon soured cream. Roll the tortilla up tightly, and place seam side down in a medium baking dish. If the *enchiladas* come unrolled, put a knife at each end to keep them in place.

When all the tortillas are rolled into *enchiladas*, cover with the remaining *Salsa*, onions, and cheese. Bake in a moderate oven, 180°C/350°F/Gas 4 for 30 minutes. Garnish with the remaining soured cream, poured over or in a separate dish.

Pollo Pibil
Baked Chicken

1–3 × 15ml spoons/1–3 tablespoons chilli powder
1 × 15ml spoon/1 tablespoon ground cumin
3 × 15ml spoons/3 tablespoons concentrated tomato purée
2 cloves of garlic, crushed
2 × 15ml spoons/2 tablespoons lime juice
4 chicken quarters
1 medium onion, thinly sliced
4 × 30cm/4 × 12 inch squares of foil

Make a paste with the chilli powder, ground cumin, tomato purée, garlic, and lime juice. Rub the paste all over each chicken quarter. Cover and chill in a refrigerator for at least 4 hours, or overnight.

Place a chicken quarter and a slice of onion on each square of foil. Fold into a packet and seal the edges of the foil. Bake on a tray in a moderate oven, 180°C/350°F/Gas 4, for 1½–2 hours, until the chicken is completely cooked. Serve the chicken, still on the foil, garnished with the remainder of the sliced onion.

Mole Poblano con Pollo
Puebla-style Chicken

Serves 12

2½kg/5 lb chicken or *turkey, poached, meat removed from the bones*
MOLE SAUCE:
3 × 15ml spoons/3 tablespoons lard
1–3 green chillies, canned or *fresh*
1 large onion, chopped
2 cloves of garlic, chopped
50g/2 oz sesame seeds
1 × 5ml spoon/1 teaspoon fennel seeds
6 coriander seeds
50g/2 oz almonds
50g/2 oz peanuts
4 black peppercorns
150ml/¼ pint chicken stock
900g/2 lb tomatoes, chopped
1 stale corn tortilla, shredded
1 × 15ml spoon/1 tablespoon ground cinnamon
2 whole cloves
1–4 × 15ml spoons/1–4 tablespoons chilli powder
50g/2 oz raisins
1 × 15ml spoon/1 tablespoon salt
50g/2 oz pumpkin seeds
50g/2 oz unsweetened chocolate
2 × 15ml spoons/2 tablespoons malt vinegar
GARNISH:
50g/2 oz toasted sesame seeds

Make the sauce first. Melt half the lard in a large saucepan. Cook the chillies, onion and garlic for 5 minutes. Add the sesame seeds, fennel seeds, coriander seeds, almonds, peanuts and peppercorns. Cook for 10 minutes. Process the mixture in a food processor, adding a small amount of chicken stock to make a smooth paste. Melt the remaining lard in the pan, and cook the tomatoes. Add the tortilla, ground cinnamon, cloves, chilli powder, raisins, salt and pumpkin seeds. Cook for 5 minutes.

Add this mixture to the bowl of the food processor, and process until smooth. Add more chicken stock if required. The *mole* paste should be quite thick now. Return all the processed mixture to the pan, and simmer, uncovered, for 45 minutes. Add the chocolate, and allow it to melt, stirring all the time. Add the vinegar and the remaining chicken stock. The sauce should now be very thick. At this point, check the seasoning. If the *mole* sauce is not spicy enough, add more chilli powder. The taste will be raw. When the sauce is cooled, store in the refrigerater. Leave for 24–48 hours. Pour about a quarter of the sauce into the bottom of a large saucepan. Add the chicken and cover with the remaining sauce. Warm gently.

Serve the chicken masked with the sauce. Sprinkle with the toasted sesame seeds.

Enchiladas de Mole
Enchiladas with Mole Sauce

8 Tortillas de Maíz *(page 14)*
corn oil for frying
300ml/½ pint Mole *sauce (page 45)*
450g/1 lb Cheddar cheese, grated
1 onion, finely chopped
GARNISH:
1 × 15ml spoon/1 tablespoon sesame seeds, toasted

Dip each tortilla into a pan of hot oil for 5 seconds, or until softened. Drain the oil from the tortilla, and immediately dip it into the *mole* sauce. Do not allow it to soak.

Arrange 25g/1 oz of cheese on the tortilla, and sprinkle some of the onion over the cheese. Roll the tortilla up tightly, and place seam side down in a medium baking dish. If the *enchiladas* come unrolled, put a knife at each end to keep them in place.

When all the tortillas are rolled into *enchiladas*, cover with the remaining sauce and onions. Top with the remaining cheese, and bake for 30 minutes in a moderate oven, 180°C/350°F/Gas 4.

If the *mole* sauce contains chicken, lift the chicken from the sauce. Use the sauce for dipping, and add the chicken to the *enchiladas* with the cheese and onions. Garnish with the toasted sesame seeds.

Tostadas de Pollo
Tostados with Chicken

¼ head iceberg lettuce, finely shredded
225g/8 oz tomatoes, chopped
Vinagreta *(page 20)*
Frijoles Refritos *(page 64)*
175g/6 oz chicken, cooked and shredded
100g/4 oz Cheddar cheese, grated
4 Tortillas de Maíz, *crisply fried (page 14)*
Guacamole *(page 20)*

Mix the lettuce and tomatoes, and dress with the *Vinagreta*.

Prepare the *Tostados* by layering a quarter of the *Frijoles Refritos*, chicken and cheese on each cooked warm tortilla. Garnish with *Guacamole* and the dressed lettuce and tomato. Serve immediately.

Tostados with Chicken

Budín de Elote Fresco
Fresh Corn Tamale Pie

12 ears of sweetcorn, fresh or *frozen*
50g/2 oz lard
3 × 15ml spoons/3 tablespoons plain white flour
1 × 5ml spoon/1 teaspoon baking powder
3 egg yolks
600ml/1 pint Mole Poblano con Pollo *(page 45), using 675g/1½ lb chicken*

Cut the sweetcorn from the cobs. Either process in a food processor, or mash with a potato masher until fairly smooth. Melt the lard in a medium pan and cook the sweetcorn for 10 minutes. Remove from the heat and add the flour, baking powder and egg yolks. Beat with a wooden spoon for 5 minutes. Pour one-half of the corn mixture into a shallow casserole. Add a layer of the *Mole Poblano con Pollo*. Complete with the other half of the corn mixture. Bake in a moderate oven, 180°C/350°F/Gas 4, for 1 hour. A cocktail stick should come out clean, when pushed all the way into the centre.

Huevos con Chorizo y Papas
Eggs with Chorizo and Potatoes

225g/8 oz chorizo
2 large potatoes, cut into 0.5cm/¼ inch cubes
½ onion, finely chopped
4 eggs

Remove the skin from the *chorizo*, and break up the meat into a medium frying pan. Cook the *chorizo* until the fat begins to run. Add the potatoes and onion, and mix well. Cover and cook for 20 minutes, or until the *chorizo* and potatoes are cooked completely.

Make four holes in the mixture with the back of a spoon. Break an egg into each hole. Cover again, and cook for a further 5 minutes, or until the eggs are cooked.

Huevos Rancheros
Ranch-style Eggs

Salsa Picante *(page 22)*
4 Tortillas de Harina, *cooked (page 16)*
Frijoles Refritos *(page 64)*
4 eggs, size 1–2

GARNISH:
100g/4 oz Cheddar cheese, grated
avocado pear, sliced

Warm the *Salsa Picante* and pour onto *warmed* plates. Top with a flour tortilla. Spread the warmed *Frijoles Refritos* on the tortilla. Keep warm. Fry the eggs; put an egg on top of the *Frijoles Refritos*. Garnish with the grated cheese and sliced avocado pear.
Serve with extra *Salsa Picante* and a bowl of chillies.

Huevos Revueltos con Frijoles
Scrambled Eggs with Beans

Frijoles Refritos *(page 64)*
Salsa Picante *(page 22)*
salt and pepper
6 eggs, size 1–2

GARNISH:
100g/4 oz Cheddar cheese, grated

Heat the beans in a medium frying pan. Make a well in the centre of the beans and add the *Salsa Picante*. Allow the *Salsa* to heat. Meanwhile, beat the eggs with the salt and pepper. Pour the eggs into the sauce, and stir until the eggs are cooked. Serve garnished with the grated cheese.

FISH & SHELLFISH

Mexico is fortunate in having an abundance of fish and shellfish. The Pacific coast, the Gulf of Mexico, the Caribbean, and the lakes and rivers produce an almost infinite choice. There are prawns, both from the Gulf and the Pacific, tuna, snapper, red snapper, turtle, lobsters, crayfish, both hard and soft shelled crabs, bass and trout, to name but a few varieties.

Fish was transported from the Mexican coast to the valleys, even in pre-Conquest days. Montezuma, who liked his fish, had it delivered every day by runners from Veracruz, on the Gulf of Mexico, to his capital, the present-day Mexico City.

The most famous fish dish served in Mexico is *Huachinango a la Veracruzana* (Red Snapper Baked in the Veracruz Style). Red snapper may not be readily available, but the sauce, made with tomatoes, onions, capers, and olives (see page 57), goes well with any firm, white-fleshed fish, or with prawns. The authentic dish features a whole fish, but if this is not possible, use fillets or steaks.

Another popular dish is *Cebiche* (page 54), fish 'cooked' in lime juice. Again, it is best made with snapper, but any firm, white-fleshed fish can be used. *Cebiche* makes a good starter, as well as a main course, especially for a summer lunch.

Veracruz-style Prawns (page 57) and *Arroz Rojo (page 69)*

Pescado en Salsa de Naranja
Fish in Orange Sauce

550g/1¼ lb white fish fillets – cod, hake or *plaice*
juice of 1 lime
1 × 15ml spoon/1 tablespoon corn oil
SAUCE:
½ × 15ml spoon/½ tablespoon corn oil
2 large tomatoes, skinned and chopped
½ onion, finely chopped
1 clove of garlic, crushed
2 × 15ml spoons/2 tablespoons chopped parsley
150ml/¼ pint fresh orange juice
GARNISH:
orange slices
green olives, stoned

Arrange the fish fillets in a foil-lined baking tray. Drizzle the lime juice and oil over the fish. Grill for 10–15 minutes, or until the fish flakes easily with a fork.

Meanwhile, make the orange sauce by lightly cooking the tomatoes, onion and garlic in the corn oil. Add the parsley and orange juice, and simmer, covered, for 5 minutes.

As each fillet of fish is served, garnish with the orange slices and olives. Pass the sauce separately.

Pescado Frito a la Campeche
Campeche-style Fried Fish

25g/1 oz plain white flour
25g/1 oz cornmeal or *polenta*
550g/1¼ lb white fish fillets
SAUCE:
1 large onion, thinly sliced
150ml/¼ pint water
150ml/¼ pint malt vinegar
a pinch of oregano
1 × 5ml spoon/1 teaspoon salt

Make the sauce first by combining all the sauce ingredients in a medium pan, and simmering until the onion is cooked. It will be transparent. Check the seasoning.

Combine the flour and cornmeal. Dip each fillet of fish in the mixture, and shallow fry until cooked and golden. Serve with the sauce.

Note This dish is a type of Mexican fish and chips.

Pescado Relleno
Stuffed Fish

1 rainbow trout or *small haddock, approximately 900g/2 lb, cleaned*
salt and pepper
juice of 1 lemon
STUFFING:
1 × 15ml spoon/1 tablespoon corn oil
¼ onion, finely chopped
225g/8 oz tomatoes, skinned and finely chopped
1 medium potato, cut into 0.5cm/¼ inch cubes
1 × 5ml spoon/1 teaspoon capers
5 almonds, chopped
1 × 5ml spoon/1 teaspoon fresh lime juice
1 × 5ml spoon/1 teaspoon salt.
freshly ground white pepper

Dust the fish with salt and pepper and the lemon juice.
Make the stuffing by heating the oil in a pan, and cooking the onion, tomatoes and potato for 5 minutes. Add the capers, almonds, lime juice and salt and pepper. Cook until the liquid disappears. Check the seasoning.
Stuff the cavity of the fish with the onion and tomato mixture. Secure the stuffing in the fish by fastening with wooden cocktail sticks. Cook in a moderate oven, 180°C/350°F/Gas 4, for 45 minutes–1 hour, until the fish flakes easily with a fork.

Cebiche
Marinated Fish

Serves 4 as a main course, or 8 as a starter

550g/1¼ lb white fish – plaice, cod, haddock, sole, monkfish, scallops, or a combination
225ml/8 fl oz fresh lime juice
75ml/3 fl oz corn oil
50ml/2 fl oz tomato ketchup
a dash of Worcestershire sauce
1 × 15ml spoon/1 tablespoon fresh coriander, chopped
salt and pepper
1 green chilli, chopped
3 tomatoes, skinned and chopped
1 medium onion, chopped
GARNISH:
1 large ear of sweetcorn
leaves of cos lettuce, shredded
green olives, stoned
sprigs of fresh coriander

Skin, debone and chop the fish into small pieces, 2.5cm/1 inch cubes. Put it into a glass bowl. (**Note** The bowl *must* be glass.) Pour the lime juice over the fish, and stir. It is essential that the fish be completely covered with the juice, as the juice 'cooks' the fish. Refrigerate for at least 8 hours. Stir occasionally.

Meanwhile, cook the ear of corn in salted boiling water for 7 minutes. Drain and cool. Cut into eight pieces. Refrigerate until ready to use.

Just before serving, drain the lime juice from the fish, reserving the juice. Put the fish to one side. Add the corn oil, tomato ketchup, Worcestershire sauce, chopped coriander, and salt and pepper to the lime juice. Mix well as for a vinaigrette.

Add the chilli, tomatoes and onion to the drained fish. Dress with the sauce made from the marinade.

Arrange the lettuce on individual serving plates, and spoon the fish mixture on top. Garnish with olives, pieces of sweetcorn and sprigs of fresh coriander.

Note *Cebiche* can be made solely with shellfish, or with a mixture of white fish and shellfish. The fish *must* be fresh.

Cebiche

Chiles Rellenos con Jaiba y Camarones
Stuffed Chillies with Crab and Prawns

Serves 4 as a main course, or 6 as a starter

12 canned green chillies, drained
550g/1¼ lb prawn and crab meat, combined
2 spring onions, chopped
150ml/¼ pint mayonnaise, made with fresh lime juice
25ml/1 fl oz fresh lime juice
GARNISH:
cos lettuce, shredded
2 jalapeño *peppers* or *Kenya chillies, deseeded and chopped*

Pat the chillies dry with kitchen paper. Combine the fish, spring onions, mayonnaise, and the lime juice. Stuff the peppers with the fish mixture. Arrange the *Chiles Rellenos* on a bed of lettuce, and sprinkle with the *jalapeño* peppers.

Note If the *jalapeño* peppers are too hot, substitute 2 green chillies.

Jaiba Mexicana
Mexican Crab

1 × 15ml spoon/1 tablespoon corn oil
2 × 15ml spoons/2 tablespoons onion, finely minced
1 red pepper, chopped
450g/1 lb fresh crab meat
6 green olives, stoned and chopped
2 × 15ml spoons/2 tablespoons capers
50g/2 oz breadcrumbs
1 × 2.5ml spoon/½ teaspoon cayenne pepper
1 hard-boiled egg, chopped
GARNISH:
lime slices

Heat the oil in a medium pan, and gently cook the onion for 5 minutes. Add the red pepper and cook for a further 5 minutes. Add the crab, olives, capers, half the breadcrumbs and the cayenne pepper. Remove from the heat, and add the chopped egg.

Either stuff 4 cleaned crab shells with the mixture, or divide among 4 small ovenproof dishes. Sprinkle the remaining breadcrumbs over the top. Bake for 25 minutes in a moderate oven, 180°C/350°F/Gas 4. Garnish with the lime slices.

Camarones en Salsa Pipián
Prawns in Pumpkin Seed Sauce

100g/4 oz pumpkin seeds
½ onion, chopped
4 tomatoes, skinned and chopped
2 × 15ml spoons/2 tablespoons concentrated tomato purée
2 green chillies
450ml/¾ pint chicken stock
3 sprigs of fresh coriander
1 × 5ml spoon/1 teaspoon salt
450g/1 lb frozen prawns, defrosted

Toast the seeds first. Heat a pan and spread the seeds over the base. Keep them moving to prevent them becoming too brown. Remove from the heat. In a food processor, or in a mortar and pestle, crush the seeds until very fine. If using a food processor, add the onion, tomatoes, tomato purée, green chillies, stock and coriander, and process. Otherwise, cook the onion in a little oil until soft. Add to the seeds with the tomatoes, tomato purée and chillies. Work until a fairly smooth consistency. Add the stock and coriander. Cook the sauce, uncovered, for 30 minutes. Check the seasoning. A little salt and pepper may be needed. Add the prawns, and simmer for 3–5 minutes, or until the prawns are just warm.

Serve with *Arroz Blanco* (page 68).

Camarones de Veracruz
Veracruz-style Prawns

2 × 15ml spoons/2 tablespoons corn oil
½ red pepper, cut into large pieces
½ green pepper, cut into large pieces
1 medium onion, roughly chopped
4 medium tomatoes, skinned and roughly chopped
2 × 15ml spoons/2 tablespoons capers
16 green olives, stoned
1 × 5ml spoon/1 teaspoon ground bay leaf
1 × 5ml spoon/1 teaspoon salt
450g/1 lb frozen prawns, defrosted

Heat the oil in a large pan with a lid. Cook the red and green peppers and the onion until soft. Add the tomatoes, capers, olives, bay leaf and salt. Cover and simmer for 25–30 minutes. Add the prawns, and heat gently for a further 3–5 minutes, or until the prawns are heated through.

Serve with either plain boiled rice or *Arroz Rojo* (page 69).

VEGETABLES, SALADS, BEANS & RICE

In all farming cultures, vegetables and grains have been the main source of food for the poor. The Mexican peasant was fortunate, because many of those vegetables and grains also provided a rich source of protein and fibre. The 50 or so varieties of beans found by the Spanish were the staple of the Indian diet, along with corn *(elote)*, and even today beans are still an important part of the Mexican diet. A pot of beans is kept on the back of the cooker for the whole week. It may begin as *Frijoles de la Olla* (page 17) and end the week as *Frijoles Refritos* (page 64), with many interesting variations in between. The same is true of chick peas.

Rice was introduced by the Conquistadores, and, like beans, is now eaten every day, both as a dry soup (see pages 68–69), vegetable and as a dessert (see *Arroz con Leche*, page 70).

Carrots, courgettes, cauliflower and *chayote* (chow chow) can all make excellent vegetarian main dishes when cooked in the Mexican style. Salads of tomatoes, lettuce, sliced avocado pear, spring onion or coriander add colour and crunch to a meal. They are usually served as a garnish to the meat course, although some, notably *Ensalada de Nochebuena* (page 66), will stand on their own as an accompaniment to any plainly grilled or roasted meat.

Salad for Christmas Eve (page 66)

Budín de Elote
Corn Pudding

450g/1 lb sweetcorn
175g/6 oz butter
3 eggs, beaten
150ml/¼ pint milk or *milk and cream combined*
1 canned green chilli, drained and chopped
salt and pepper

Combine all the ingredients in a medium soufflé dish, or process in a food processor until you have a creamy mixture. Season to taste.
Cook in a bain marie in a moderate oven, 180°C/350°F/Gas 4, for 30–45 minutes. The pudding is done when a knife comes out of the centre clean.

Variation
For a spicier pudding, substitute a *jalapeño* or Kenya chilli for the green chilli.

Budín de Calabacitas
Courgette Pudding

450g/1 lb courgettes, cut into 2.5cm/1 inch slices
25g/1 oz butter
¼ onion, finely chopped
1 clove of garlic, crushed
450g/1 lb tomatoes, skinned and chopped
50g/2 oz Lancashire cheese, grated
4 eggs, separated

Cook the courgettes in boiling salted water for 5 minutes, then drain well. Melt the butter in a pan, and soften the onion and garlic. Remove from the heat, and add the tomatoes, courgettes and cheese. Mix well.
Meanwhile, beat the egg whites until stiff. Mix in the egg yolks, then fold in the courgette mixture. Pour into a buttered medium soufflé dish, and bake in a moderate oven, 180°C/350°F/Gas 4, for 45 minutes.

Calabacita
Courgettes, Corn and Peppers

1½ × 15ml spoons/1½ tablespoons lard
250g/9 oz courgettes, sliced
150g/5 oz fresh or *frozen sweetcorn*
¼ red pepper, cut into 2.5cm/1 inch pieces
¼ green pepper, cut into 2.5cm/1 inch pieces
½ medium onion, finely chopped
1 clove of garlic, crushed
2 pinches of dried oregano
100g/4 oz tomatoes, skinned and chopped
salt and pepper
GARNISH:
sprigs of coriander

Melt the lard in a heavy pan. Add the vegetables and seasonings. Cook for approximately 7 minutes, or until the vegetables are done. Season to taste. Garnish with the fresh coriander.

Calabacitas de Casa
Home-style Courgettes

450g/1 lb courgettes, cut into 2.5cm/1 inch slices
1 medium onion, thinly sliced
2 cloves of garlic, crushed
2 × 15ml spoons/2 tablespoons fresh coriander, chopped
4 canned green chillies, drained and chopped
1 × 5ml spoon/1 teaspoon salt

Combine all the ingredients in a large pan, cover, and cook over low heat for 15–20 minutes. Stir occasionally. The vegetables should cook in their own liquid. If they seem too dry, add 1 × 15ml spoon/1 tablespoon of water. Do not overcook. The courgettes should still have a 'bite'.

Chayotes Rellenos
Stuffed Chayote

4 chayote *(chow chow)*
1 × 15ml spoon/1 tablespoon corn oil
1 small onion, finely chopped
1 clove of garlic, crushed
1 large tomato, skinned and chopped
2 eggs, beaten
100g/4 oz Emmental cheese, grated
8 × 15ml spoons/8 tablespoons Parmesan cheese

Cook the *chayote* by covering them with boiling salted water and boiling gently for 20–30 minutes. Test with a small skewer. Drain.

Cut each *chayote* in half, and scoop out the seed with a small spoon. Discard the seed, or chop and use to garnish. Scoop out the flesh, leaving the skin and about 1.25cm/½ inch of flesh. Chop the flesh.

Heat the oil in a pan, and cook the onion and garlic for 5 minutes. Add the tomato, and cook for a further 5 minutes.

In a bowl, combine the beaten eggs, *chayote* flesh, cooked onion, garlic, tomatoes and Emmental cheese.

Fill each *chayote* half with one-eighth of the mixture. Top with 1 × 15ml spoon/1 tablespoon of grated Parmesan cheese. Cook for 30 minutes in a moderate oven, 180°C/350°F/Gas 4.

Chayote con Crema y Queso
Chayote with Cream and Cheese

2 chayote *(chow chow), cooked*
salt and pepper
100ml/4fl oz single cream
50g/2 oz Parmesan cheese, grated
sprigs of coriander, chopped

Split the cooked *chayote* in half. Peel and scoop out the seed, reserving it for the garnish. Slice the *chayote* thickly, and arrange in a buttered ovenproof dish. Lightly dust with salt and pepper, spoon over the cream, and finish off by covering with the cheese. Bake in a moderate oven, 180°C/350°F/Gas 4, for 30 minutes. Brown the cheese lightly under the grill. Garnish with chopped coriander and the chopped seeds from the *chayote*.

Stuffed Chayote

Frijoles Negros
Black Beans

225g/8 oz black beans
1 medium onion, chopped
3 × 15ml spoons/3 tablespoons lard
4 spring onions, chopped
1 jalapeño *pepper* or *1 Kenya chilli, chopped*
2 tomatoes, skinned and chopped
2 × 5ml spoons/2 teaspoons salt
pepper
GARNISH:
chopped coriander
Salsa Verde *(page 21)*

Cover the beans with water, and soak overnight. Drain off the soaking water and rinse. Cover the beans with fresh water in a large pan. Bring to a boil and boil briskly for 15 minutes. Drain the beans, and cover with fresh water. Add the onion and 1 × 5ml spoon/1 teaspoon of lard. Bring to a boil and cook until soft. This will take approximately 2 hours.

Meanwhile, cook the spring onion and the *jalapeño* pepper in the remainder of the lard.

When the beans are cooked, add the onion and pepper mixture and the tomatoes. Mix and mash well. Add the salt and pepper, mix, and check the seasoning. Serve sprinkled with the chopped coriander and *Salsa Verde*.

Frijoles Refritos
Refried Beans

75g/3 oz lard
1 large onion, finely chopped
1 clove of garlic, crushed
Frijoles de la Olla *(page 17), drained, liquid reserved*
75g/3 oz Cheddar cheese, grated

Melt 25g/1 oz of lard in a heavy based pan. Cook the onion and the garlic until soft. Add the drained *Frijoles*. Mash either with a potato masher, or with the back of a wooden spoon.

When the beans are completely mashed, add a small amount of the liquid from the beans and mix, then add 1 × 15ml spoon/1 tablespoon of lard. Allow to cook. When almost dry, repeat the addition of the liquid and the lard. Continue to cook until the liquid and the lard are used. Serve the beans garnished with the grated Cheddar cheese.

Ensalada de Garbanzos
Chick Pea Salad

175g/6 oz dried chick peas
50ml/2 fl oz corn oil
50ml/2 fl oz red wine vinegar
1 × 15ml spoon/1 tablespoon chopped parsley
6 spring onions
¼ red pepper, chopped
¼ green pepper, chopped
12 green olives, stoned

Soak the chick peas in water overnight. Drain, and discard the water. Cover the chick peas with fresh water, and bring to a boil. Boil briskly for 15 minutes. Drain the chick peas, and cover with fresh water. Bring back to a boil, and simmer until the chick peas are just tender. This will take approximately 45 minutes. Do not overcook.

When the chick peas are cooked, strain off the cooking liquid. Pour the oil, and vinegar over them, and mix. Add the parsley and mix again, set aside and allow to cool.

When the chick peas are cooled completely, add the onions, red and green pepper and olives, and mix so that the vegetables are well distributed. Cover and refrigerate. Serve well chilled.

Ensalada de Coliflor
Cauliflower Salad

1 medium cauliflower, divided into florets
DRESSING:
75ml/3 fl oz corn oil
50ml/2 fl oz white wine vinegar
1 × 15ml spoon/1 tablespoon parsley, chopped
1 × 15ml spoon/1 tablespoon red pepper, chopped
2 × 15ml spoons/2 tablespoons hard-boiled egg white, chopped
a pinch of salt
GARNISH:
fresh coriander

Cook the cauliflower florets in boiling water until just tender, about 3-4 minutes. Drain.

Make the dressing by combining the remaining ingredients in a glass jar, and shaking vigorously. Check the seasoning, and add more salt if needed.

Put the cooked cauliflower into a covered bowl, and pour over the dressing. Chill for at least 2 hours. Garnish with the coriander.

Ensalada de Bandera Mexicana
Mexican Flag Salad

225g/8 oz sweetcorn, either canned or *frozen, cooked with 1 × 2.5ml spoon/½ teaspoon sugar*
100ml/4 fl oz Vinagreta *(page 20)*
¼ onion, chopped
¼ red pepper, chopped
Guacamole *(page 20)*
seeds from ½ pomegranate
tortilla chips

Cook the corn in the boiling water for 4–5 minutes. The kernels of corn should be cooked, but still have a 'bite'. Drain the corn well, then mix the *Vinagreta* into the corn, and allow to cool. When the corn is cooled, mix in the onion and pepper. Refrigerate until ready for use.
Just before serving, make the *Guacamole*. Drain any excess *Vinagreta* from the corn. Arrange the corn mixture across the centre third of a serving plate. Spread the *Guacamole* on either side. Sprinkle the pomegranate seeds over the corn and the *Guacamole*. Serve with the tortilla chips arranged around the edge of the plate.

Ensalada de Nochebuena
Salad for Christmas Eve

6 large leaves of cos lettuce
4 medium beetroot, cooked, peeled and thinly sliced
2 medium dessert apples, sliced
1 orange, in segments
3 × 15ml spoons/3 tablespoons fresh lime or *lemon juice*
2 bananas, sliced
4 carrots, cooked and sliced
1–2 slices fresh pineapple (optional)
1 × 2.5ml spoon/½ tablespoon unsalted peanuts
1 × 2.5ml spoon/½ tablespoon pine nuts
seeds from 1 pomegranate
DRESSING:
250ml/9 fl oz corn oil
75ml/3 fl oz fresh lime or *lemon juice*
1 × 5ml spoon/1 teaspoon clear honey
salt and pepper

Arrange the lettuce leaves on a serving plate, then arrange, in a semi-circle, the slices of beetroot, apple, orange, banana, carrot and pineapple, if using. Just before serving, scatter the nuts and pomegranate seeds over the salad. Make the dressing by combining all the ingredients, ensuring that the honey is mixed in well. Serve separately.

Mexican Flag Salad

Arroz Blanco
White Rice

2 × 15ml spoons/2 tablespoons corn oil
1 onion, finely chopped
1 clove of garlic, crushed
1 Kenya chilli, de-seeded and chopped
175g/6 oz long grain white rice
475ml/16 fl oz chicken stock
2 × 5ml spoons/2 teaspoons salt

Heat the corn oil in a flameproof casserole, and cook the onion, garlic and chilli until lightly browned. Add the rice, and brown. When the rice is browned, add the chicken stock and salt. Bring to a boil. Cover, and steam in a moderate oven, 180°C/350°F/Gas 4, for 30 minutes. Remove from the oven, and stir with a fork to separate the grains of rice.

Arroz Mexicano
Mexican-style Rice

2 × 15ml spoons/2 tablespoons corn oil
1 small onion, finely chopped
1 clove of garlic, crushed
1 large carrot, finely chopped
175g/6 oz long grain rice
475ml/16 fl oz chicken stock
2 large tomatoes, skinned and chopped
50g/2 oz peas
2 × 5ml spoons/2 teaspoons salt

Heat the oil in a flameproof casserole. Cook the onion, garlic and carrot until lightly browned. Add the rice, and brown. When the rice is browned, add the chicken stock and bring to a boil. Add the tomatoes, peas and salt. Cover, and steam in a moderate oven, 180°C/350°F/Gas 4 for 30 minutes. Remove from the oven, and stir with a fork to separate the grains of rice.

Arroz Rojo
Red Rice

2 × 15ml spoons/2 tablespoons corn oil
175g/6 oz white long grain rice
1 small onion, chopped
1 clove of garlic, crushed
475ml/16 fl oz chicken stock
4 medium tomatoes, skinned and roughly chopped
2 × 15ml spoons/2 tablespoons concentrated tomato purée
1 × 5ml spoon/1 teaspoon salt

Heat the oil in a flameproof casserole. Lightly brown the rice. Add the onion and garlic, and continue to cook until the onion is softened. Add the stock, tomatoes, tomato purée and salt. Bring to a boil. Cover, and cook in a moderate oven, 180°C/350°F/Gas 4, for 30 minutes. Remove from the oven, and stir with a fork to separate the grains of rice.

Arroz Verde
Green Rice

2 × 15ml spoons/2 tablespoons corn oil
1 medium onion, chopped
1 clove of garlic, crushed
1 Kenya chilli, de-seeded and chopped
½ green pepper, finely chopped
175g/6 oz long grain white rice
475ml/16 fl oz chicken stock
2 × 5ml spoons/2 teaspoons salt
4 × 15ml spoons/4 tablespoons fresh coriander, chopped

Heat the oil in a flameproof casserole, and cook the onion, garlic and Kenya chilli until browned. Add the green pepper and rice. Brown the rice. Add the chicken stock, salt and coriander. Bring to a boil. Cover, and steam in a moderate oven, 180°C/350°F/Gas 4, for 30 minutes. Remove from the oven, and stir with a fork to separate the grains of rice.

DESSERTS & BREADS

After what can be a fiery meal, something soothing is in order. Nursery-like milk, rice and bread puddings appear frequently on the Mexican menu. If these are too bland for your taste, choose from the tropical fruits found in abundance in every market. Use pineapples, mangoes, guavas, and papayas in sorbets, mousses, fruit salads, to top ice cream, or simply serve on their own.

More substantial desserts include sweet *tamales*, cakes and sweet breads. The French influence is still to be seen in the pastries and breads produced by Mexican bakeries, and *Capirotada* (page 72) requires a French-style bread as a base.

One of the delights of Mexican cooking is that nothing is ever wasted. Left-over bread is used for a special pudding for Lent (page 72). Left-over *Rompope* (page 86) is used as the base for a mousse (page 73). If there is any *maíz* left over from making *tamales*, it can be sweetened and wrapped round pineapple to become *Tamales de Piña* (page 71) or wrapped around any dried fruits – raisins, apricots, peaches – to become a *tamal dulce* (sweet tamale).

Arroz con Leche
Rice Pudding

175g/6 oz long grain white rice
450ml/¾ pint water
a pinch of salt
450ml/¾ pint milk, scalded
100g/4 oz caster sugar or *vanilla sugar*
2 egg yolks
50g/2 oz sultanas
DECORATION:
ground cinnamon

Cook the rice, covered, in the salted water for 10 minutes, or until the water is almost completely absorbed. Add the milk, sugar and egg yolks, and continue to cook over a low heat until the liquid is absorbed and the rice is creamy and thick, but not dry. Stir in the sultanas. Pour into a serving bowl and sprinkle the cinnamon over. Serve warm.

Tamales de Piña
Pineapple Tamales

Makes 16

275g/10 oz masa harina
1 × 5ml spoon/1 teaspoon baking powder
225g/8 oz dark brown sugar
75ml/3 fl oz corn oil
350ml/12 fl oz pineapple juice mixed with water
225g/8 oz canned crushed pineapple, drained
16 dried corn husks or *16 pieces of foil, 15cm × 20cm/6 inches × 8 inches*
175g/6 oz glacé pineapple, finely chopped

Mix the *masa harina*, baking powder and 175g/6 oz sugar together. Gradually mix with the oil alternating with the pineapple juice and water. Beat in the crushed pineapple.

Drain the husks, if using, and dry between two tea-towels. Spread the husks or foil on a work surface. Divide the dough among the husks/foil. Spread the dough into a rectangular form, leaving a 2.5cm/1 inch strip down one long side. Sprinkle on 1 × 5ml spoon/1 teaspoon brown sugar, then divide the glacé pineapple among the 16 *tamales*. Fold over the long side of the husks/foil, then fold the narrow half over to make a packet open at one end.

Continue as on page 18, but steam the *tamales* for 1 hour only.

Serve with *Salsa de Piña* if desired.

Salsa de Piña
Pineapple Sauce

375g/13 oz canned crushed pineapple or *fresh pineapple*
25g/1 oz light brown sugar
1 × 15ml spoon/1 tablespoon dark rum or *brandy*

Combine the pineapple, sugar and rum or brandy in a small pan. Simmer gently until slightly thickened.

Serve with *Tamales de Piña* or as a topping for vanilla ice cream.

Capirotada
Bread Pudding for Lent

450g/1 lb stale French loaf, cut in 2.5cm/
1 inch slices
75g/3 oz butter
25g/1 oz almonds, chopped
75g/3 oz sultanas
100g/4 oz cream cheese
SYRUP:
350g/12 oz dark brown sugar
1 cinnamon stick
1 × 2.5ml spoon/½ teaspoon anise seeds

Make the syrup first by combining the brown sugar, stick of cinnamon and anise seeds, and simmering in a heavy based pan for 20 minutes. Set aside and cool. When cooled, strain off the cinnamon stick and anise seeds.
Butter the bread with 50g/2 oz of the butter. In a large ovenproof dish, layer half the buttered bread, half the almonds, half the sultanas and half the cream cheese. Pour half the syrup over. Add another layer in the same order. Pour the remaining syrup over. Dot the remaining butter over the top. Bake in a moderate oven, 180°C/350°F/Gas 4, for 45 minutes. Allow to stand for at least 30 minutes before serving.

Flan de Café
Coffee Crème Caramel

225g/8 oz sugar
2 eggs
2 egg yolks
300ml/½ pint single cream
400g/14 oz canned sweetened condensed milk
2 × 5ml spoons/2 teaspoons coffee powder

Caramelize the sugar in a heavy based pan. Pour into a medium ovenproof casserole or bowl. Rotate so that the bowl or casserole is coated with the caramel.
Beat the eggs and egg yolks in a bowl until creamy. Add the cream, sweetened condensed milk and coffee. Stir until the coffee powder is dissolved.
Pour into the bowl or casserole, and cook in a bain marie in a moderate oven, 180°C/350°F/Gas 4, for 1¼ hours, or until a knife inserted into the centre comes out clean.
Remove the casserole from the bain marie, and cool. When cool, refrigerate until well chilled, and unmould.

Mousse de Rompope
Eggnog Mousse

Serves 8

1 × 15ml spoon/1 tablespoon gelatine
50ml/2 fl oz water
300ml/½ pint Rompope *(page 86)*
150ml/¼ pint whipping cream
4 egg whites

DECORATION:
whipped cream, sweetened with a little caster sugar
8 strawberries (optional)

In a small bowl, soften the gelatine in the water for 5 minutes. Place the bowl in a shallow pan of warm water, and stir until the gelatine is clear and dissolved. Combine the gelatine and water with the *Rompope*. Chill for 10–15 minutes, until the mixture is like very thick cream. Do not allow to set. Whip the cream until stiff. In another bowl, beat the egg whites until they stand in peaks. Fold the cream into the *Rompope* and gelatine, then fold in the egg whites. Pour into individual ramekins, or into a medium soufflé dish. Chill. Serve topped with whipped, sweetened cream and a fresh strawberry.

Cajeta
Burned Milk Sauce

400g/14 oz canned sweetened condensed milk

Cover the unopened can of milk with water in a large pan. Bring the water to a boil, and simmer for 2 hours. It is essential that the can of milk be covered with water the whole time. Remove the can from the water, and cool. Refrigerate until ready to use.

Use as a topping for ice cream, or as a butterscotch-type sauce over cooked apples or pears.

Note This sauce is made with goat's milk in Mexico.

Sorbete de Lima
Lime Sorbet

8 limes
350g/12 oz sugar
200ml/⅓ pint water
200ml/⅓ pint fresh lime juice (8 limes)
2 egg whites

Pare/grate the rind from four of the limes. Bring the sugar, water and rind to a boil. Simmer for 15 minutes. Remove from the heat and cool completely. Squeeze the juice from the limes. When the sugar syrup has cooled, sieve to remove the lime rind from the syrup. Combine with the lime juice, and freeze in a freezer-resistant glass bowl for 45 minutes, or until a heavy, syrupy consistency.

Beat the egg whites until stiff. Fold them into the mixture, and freeze.

Galletas de Boda
Wedding Cakes

Makes 36 (approx)

100g/4 oz butter
250g/9 oz caster sugar
100g/4 oz plain white flour
150g/5 oz walnuts, finely chopped
1 × 5ml spoon/1 teaspoon vanilla flavouring
a pinch of salt
red food colouring (optional)
green food colouring (optional)

Cream together the butter and 25g/1 oz of the sugar until light. Sieve in the flour and mix. Add the walnuts, vanilla flavouring and salt. Mix until well blended.

At this point, the dough can be divided into three equal portions. Colour one portion red, and another portion green. Use only 2–3 drops of each colour. Roll the dough into 2.5cm/1 inch balls. Place on a lightly oiled baking sheet. Bake in a moderate oven, 180°C/350°F/Gas 4, for 15 minutes. Remove from the oven, and roll in the remaining sugar. Cool on a wire rack.

Note If the cakes are not coloured, they are wedding cakes. The whiteness represents the purity of the bride. The green, white and red cakes represent the colours of the Mexican flag.

Wedding Cakes

Buñuelos
Sweet Fried Pastries

Makes 12

175g/6 oz plain white flour
1 × 15ml spoon/1 tablespoon sugar
½ × 2.5ml spoon/¼ teaspoon baking powder
½ × 2.5ml spoon/¼ teaspoon salt
1 egg, beaten
100ml/4 fl oz milk
25g/1 oz butter, melted
100g/4 oz caster sugar
1 × 5ml spoon/1 teaspoon ground cinnamon
corn oil for frying

Sieve the flour, the tablespoon of sugar, baking powder and salt together into a medium bowl.

Mix the egg and milk together. Add the melted butter. Add the milk and butter to the flour mixture, and mix into a smooth dough. Turn out on to a floured surface, and knead for 5 minutes, or until a smooth, stretchy dough.

Divide into 12 balls of dough. Cover with a dry tea-towel and leave for 30 minutes.

Meanwhile, combine the caster sugar and cinnamon in a separate bowl. Put one of the balls of dough on to a floured surface, and pat out into a circle. Stretch the dough to make it as thin as possible. Continue with the remaining balls of dough.

Heat a pan of oil to 180°C/350°F. Fry each *buñuelo* in the oil until golden. Turn only once. Drain on kitchen paper. Sprinkle the hot *buñuelos* with the cinnamon sugar.

Note The *buñuelos* will keep for a few days in an airtight container, but are best freshly made.

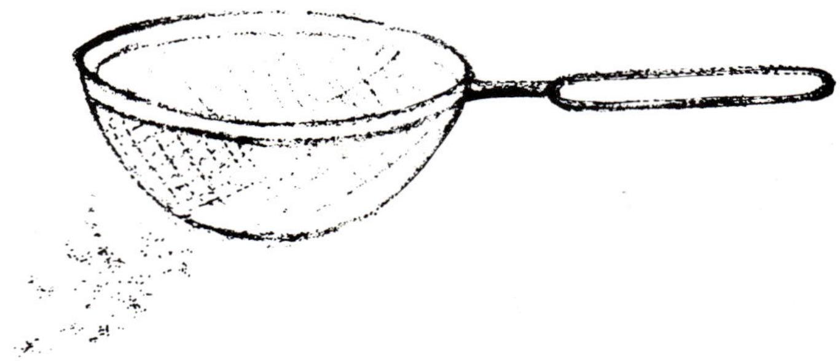

Sopapillas
Fried Pastries in Syrup

Makes 9

225g/8 oz plain white flour
1 × 2.5ml spoon/½ teaspoon salt
2 × 15ml spoons/2 teaspoons baking powder
1 × 15ml spoon/1 tablespoon butter
150ml/¼ pint warm water
corn oil for frying

SYRUP:
3 × 15ml spoons/3 tablespoons clear honey
1 × 5ml spoon/1 teaspoon ground cinnamon
1 × 15ml spoon/1 tablespoon butter
1 × 15ml spoon/1 tablespoon brandy

Sieve together the flour, salt and baking powder. Rub in the butter. Add the warm water, and work into a soft dough. Turn out on to a floured surface, and knead for 5 minutes. Return the dough to the bowl, and cover with a dry tea-towel. Leave to rest for 30 minutes.

Meanwhile, make the syrup by combining the honey, cinnamon, butter and brandy. Simmer gently for 5 minutes. Keep warm.

Turn the dough out on to a floured surface, and roll into a 20cm/8 inch square. Cut it into nine pieces. Let the dough rest again for 5 minutes.

Heat a pan of oil to 180°C/350°F. Fry each *sopapilla* until golden and puffed. Turn only once. If the *sopapillas* do not puff, the oil is not hot enough. Remove the *sopapillas* when cooked, and drain on kitchen paper. Keep warm.

When all are fried, arrange on a plate and pour the warmed syrup over. Eat while still warm.

Serve with *Café a la Mexicana* (page 85).

Pan de Muerto
Bread for the Dead

600ml/1 pint milk
25g/1 oz fresh yeast or *1 × 15ml spoon/1 tablespoon dried yeast*
900g/2 lb strong white flour, sieved
1 × 5ml spoon/1 teaspoon salt
beaten egg
2 × 15ml spoons/2 tablespoons caster sugar

Warm the milk to blood temperature. Blend the fresh yeast into the warm milk, or reconstitute the dried yeast. Add one-quarter of the flour. Mix and leave for 10 minutes. The yeast mixture will be foaming at the top.

Mix the salt into the remaining flour. Add the yeast mixture, and mix until it is a smooth dough. Turn out on to a floured surface, and knead for 10 minutes. Return the dough to the bowl, cover with a damp tea-towel, and leave to rise in a warm place for 2 hours.

When the dough has doubled in bulk, knock it back and divide it into two equal portions for two loaves. Tear off and reserve about one-sixth of the dough from each portion.

Prepare a baking tray by brushing with either corn oil or butter.

Form the two large portions of dough into two round loaves. Place the two loaves on the prepared baking tray.

Divide the two smaller portions of dough into two pieces, giving four pieces of dough of equal size. Roll the pieces into ropes approximately 15cm/6 inches long. Flatten the ends of each rope. The rope should now look like a bone with 'knuckles' at each end.

Brush the two loaves of bread with the beaten egg. Over each loaf cross the two 'bones', then brush the loaves with more beaten egg. Cover with a damp tea-towel until doubled in bulk. This will take approximately 45 minutes. When the dough has doubled in bulk, sprinkle half the sugar over each loaf. Bake in a hot oven, 220°C/425°F/Gas 7, for about 40 minutes or until well browned. Remove from the tray and cool on a rack.

Bread for the Dead

Rosca de Reyes
Ring of the Kings

225g/8 oz strong white flour
a pinch of salt
25g/1 oz lard
15g/½ oz fresh yeast or *½ × 15ml spoon/ ½ tablespoon dried yeast*
5 × 15ml spoons/5 tablespoons cold water
25g/1 oz sugar
2 eggs
75g/3 oz candied mixed peel
50g/2 oz currants
caster sugar

Sieve the flour and salt into a large bowl, and rub in the lard.

Blend the yeast with half the water, or reconstitute the dried yeast. Mix together the 25g/1 oz of sugar and one egg, and add to the yeast liquid. Make a well in the flour, pour in the yeast mixture, and mix well with the rest of the water until a soft dough is formed. Beat well until smooth. Knead the dough for 10 minutes.

Roll into a rectangle approximately 15cm/6 inches wide and 45cm/18 inches long. Sprinkle the candied peel and the currants down the centre of the rectangle. Fold the two long sides to the centre, and seal with a little of the remaining egg, beaten. Place the rolled dough on a baking tray, seam side down, and form into a ring. Cover with a slightly damp tea-towel, and leave in a warm place until doubled in size, approximately 30–45 minutes.

Brush the ring with the beaten egg, and lightly sprinkle the caster sugar over. Bake in a hot oven, 220°C/425°F/Gas 7, for 30–35 minutes.

Note This bread is especially good served with *Café a la Mexicana* (page 85).

DRINKS & COCKTAIL SAVOURIES

Mexico is heaven for the thirsty, from morning to night. The day starts with a steaming cup of coffee, from the states of Oaxaca, Chiapas and Veracruz, and ends with hot chocolate, made Mexican style with cinnamon and vanilla (page 84). Street vendors in every town and village sell deliciously refreshing fruit drinks made from fresh fruit blended with ice and sugar, or ice, sugar and milk (see below).

Kahlúa is Mexico's favourite liqueur. Based on coffee, brandy, cocoa and vanilla, it can be mixed with vodka or cream, or drunk on its own. Both dark and light rums are also produced, and are the base of *Rompope* (page 86), made with eggs and milk.

Antojitos (little savouries) are served with drinks before a meal. These range from *Pepitas* (page 90), nuts and *Totopos* (page 16) to a variety of tasty dips made with beans, cheese and chillies (pages 92–93) and served with *Totopos* or tortilla chips.

Bebidas Frutas Mixtas
Blender Fruit Drinks

Makes three 150ml/¼ pint drinks

300ml/½ pint prepared and chopped fruit – pineapple, strawberries, bananas, melon
2 × 15ml spoons/2 tablespoons icing sugar
300ml/½ pint cold milk
DECORATION:
fresh fruit

Fill a blender cup with shaved or crushed ice. Add the fruit, sugar and milk. Blend for 30 seconds. The mixture will be slushy. Pour into tall glasses and decorate with slices of fruit.

Sangría de Xochimilco
Lime Sangria Float

Serves 1

---

1 × 15ml spoon/1 tablespoon sugar
1 × 15ml spoon/1 tablespoon water
25ml/1 fl oz fresh lime juice
75ml/3 fl oz sparkling water or *soda water*
150ml/¼ pint red wine
DECORATION:
slice of lime

Heat together the sugar and water until boiling, then leave to cool. Combine with the lime juice and water in a tall glass. Add 4–5 ice cubes. Carefully pour in the red wine. The lime mixture will be on the bottom and the red wine will float above it. Serve with a slice of lime and a straw.

Besito de Kahlúa
Kahlúa Kiss

Serves 1

50ml/2 fl oz Kahlúa
1 × 15ml spoon/1 tablespoon double cream

Pour the Kahlúa into a small wine glass. Add the cream. The Kahlúa will boil up and 'kiss' the cream, and then mix of its own accord. Drink immediately.

A Selection of Mexican Drinks
Lime Sangria Float, Kahlua Kiss and *Blender Fruit Drink (page 81)*

Limada
Limeade

Makes 1.3 litres/2¼ pints (approx)

225g/8 oz sugar
1 litre/1¾ pints water
300ml/½ pint fresh lime juice (10–12 limes)

DECORATION:
lime slices

Heat together the sugar and 300ml/½ pint water until boiling, then leave to cool.

In a jug combine the sugar syrup, the remaining water and the lime juice. Serve in tall glasses and decorate with a slice of lime.

Variation

Fill a blender cup with shaved ice, 150ml/¼ pint of the fresh lime juice and half the sugar syrup, and blend. The result will be similar to the fruit slushes sold by vendors in Mexican markets.

Chocolate a la Mexicana
Mexican Chocolate

50g/2 oz unsweetened chocolate, grated
25g/1 oz vanilla sugar
2 × 5ml spoons/2 teaspoons ground cinnamon
750ml/1¼ pints milk

Combine the chocolate, vanilla sugar, cinnamon and milk in a medium saucepan. Place over a saucepan of hot water, and heat gently until the chocolate is melted and mixed well into the milk. Serve warm.

Café a la Mexicana
Mexican Coffee

4 × 15ml spoons/4 tablespoons cocoa powder
4 × 15ml spoons/4 tablespoons Demerara sugar
4 cinnamon sticks
600ml/1 pint hot coffee, preferably made with Mexican coffee beans

In 4 mugs or cups, put 1 × 15ml spoon/1 tablespoon cocoa powder and 1 × 15ml spoon/1 tablespoon Demerara sugar. Mix well. Stand a cinnamon stick in each mug or cup. Pour the hot coffee over the cocoa and sugar, using the cinnamon stick to stir. If you do not have cinnamon sticks, substitute 1 × 5ml spoon/1 teaspoon ground cinnamon, and combine with the cocoa and the sugar.

Café de Kahlúa
Kahlúa Coffee

Serves 1

4 × 5ml spoons/4 teaspoons cocoa powder
4 × 5ml spoons/4 teaspoons ground cinnamon
hot coffee
25ml/1 fl oz Kahlúa or *other coffee flavoured liqueur*

DECORATION:
whipped cream, sweetened

Combine the cocoa powder and ground cinnamon in a mug or cup. Pour about 25ml/1 fl oz hot coffee over the cocoa powder and cinnamon. Mix well to dissolve the dry ingredients. Add the Kahlúa or other coffee liqueur. Top up with the hot coffee. Decorate with the whipped cream.

Rompope
Eggnog

Makes 1 litre/1¾ pints

750ml/1¼ pints milk
350g/12 oz granulated sugar
1 vanilla pod
4 egg yolks
175ml/6 fl oz white rum

Simmer the milk, sugar and vanilla pod in a large pan for 30 minutes. Remove from the heat, and allow to cool completely.

Meanwhile, beat the egg yolks in a small bowl until a light lemon colour. When the milk mixture is completely cooled, remove the vanilla pod. Beat in the egg yolks. Return to the heat and bring just to boiling point. The mixture will begin to bubble and move around the edges. Remove from the heat immediately. It is essential that the mixture is not allowed to boil. Cool again. Add the white rum.

Bottle and refrigerate. Use after 2 days. Serve as an after-dinner drink, or over fruit as a dessert, or as a base for a mousse (page 73).

Note The *Rompope* will keep for several weeks in the refrigerator.

Variation

Rompope also makes a good drink for a holiday party. Make it the week before and serve from a punch bowl. Decorate with fresh nutmeg and whipped cream.

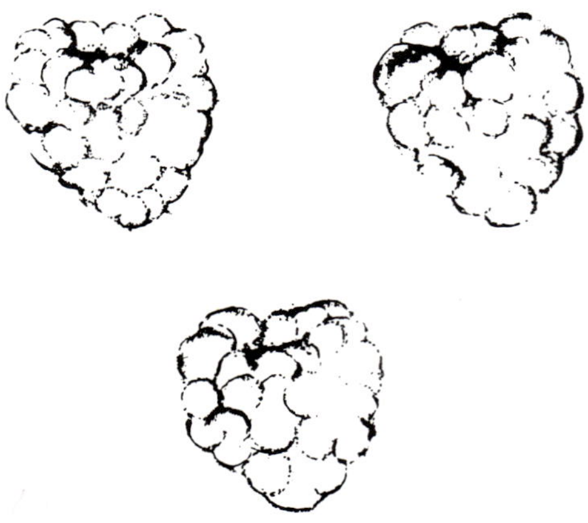

Sangría Blanca
White Sangria

2 juicy oranges, finely sliced
2 lemons, finely sliced
2 limes, finely sliced
225g/8 oz caster sugar
225g/8 oz soft fruit (raspberries or *strawberries)*
150ml/¼ pint white tequila
1 × 75cl/25 fl oz bottle German, or *similar, white wine*
1 × 75cl/25 fl oz bottle sparkling white wine, or *lemonade*

Put the orange, lemon and lime slices in a glass punch bowl. Cover with the sugar. Press the fruit with the back of a large spoon so that the juice runs. Stir until the sugar is dissolved in the juice. Add the soft fruit. If fresh fruit is not available, frozen, defrosted raspberries will be a good substitute.

When ready to serve the punch, pour the tequila and white wine over the fruit. At the table, finish off with the sparkling wine or lemonade. Serve with ice cubes.

Licor de Café
Coffee Liqueur

50g/2 oz freeze dried coffee granules
800g/1¾ lb granulated sugar
225ml/8 fl oz boiling water
1 vanilla pod, cut into four pieces
1 litre/1¾ pints brandy
450ml/¾ pint vodka

Dissolve the coffee and sugar in the boiling water. Do not heat. Stir until the coffee and sugar are dissolved. Allow to cool.

In a very large jar – a glass sweet jar would be ideal – combine the coffee mixture and the vanilla pod, brandy and vodka. Allow to stand for 30 days. After 30 days decant the liqueur into smaller bottles.

Chile con Queso
Chillies with Cheese

2 × 15ml spoons/2 tablespoons corn oil
1 medium onion, finely chopped
1 green pepper, finely chopped
1 clove of garlic, crushed
225g/8 oz tomatoes, skinned and chopped or *225g/8oz canned tomatoes*
100g/4 oz canned green chillies, drained and chopped
450g/1 lb cheese, processed, Emmental, Cheddar or *a mixture, grated*
1 × 2.5ml spoon/½ teaspoon salt
150ml/¼ pint soured cream
Tabasco sauce (optional)

Heat the oil in a pan, and cook the onion, pepper and garlic until the onion is lightly browned. Add the tomatoes, and cook for 2 minutes. Add the chillies, and heat through. Slowly add the cheese, stirring all the time. This must be done over a low heat to prevent the cheese from catching and burning. When the cheese is completely melted, make sure the cooked vegetables are well distributed through the mixture. Add the salt. At this point you may cool and refrigerate the cheese mixture.

To serve, heat the cheese slowly, add the soured cream and mix well. Check to see if the *Chile con Queso* has enough 'heat'. If it does not, add the Tabasco, drop by drop, until hot enough. Serve in a flameproof dish, kept warm on a hot plate or over a candle.

Serve with *Totopos* (page 16), corn chips or tortilla chips.

Nachos
Crispy Cheese Snacks

Totopos *(page 16)*
225g/8 oz Cheddar cheese, grated
4 jalapeño *peppers* or *Kenya chillies sliced into rings*

Spread the *totopos* on a baking sheet. The chips will overlap. Sprinkle on the grated cheese, and then the *jalapeño* peppers. Grill until the cheese is melted.

Serve immediately with *Salsa Picante* (page 22) and *Guacamole* (page 29), with dips (pages 92–93).

Empanadas
Hot Meat Turnovers

Makes 24

FILLING:
450g/1 lb minced beef
2 × 15ml spoons/2 tablespoons corn oil
1 clove of garlic, crushed
½ medium onion, finely chopped
1–6 × 5ml spoons/1–6 teaspoons chilli powder
½ × 15ml spoon/½ tablespoon ground cumin
3 × 15ml spoons/3 tablespoons concentrated tomato purée
1 × 5ml spoon/1 teaspoon salt
150ml/¼ pint water
1 hard-boiled egg, chopped
25g/1 oz raisins, chopped
PASTRY:
225g/8 oz butter
225g/8 oz cream cheese
225g/8 oz plain flour
1 × 2.5ml spoon/½ teaspoon salt

Make the filling first. Brown the beef in the oil in a medium pan. As it cooks, break it up into small pieces. Add the garlic, onion, chilli powder, ground cumin, tomato purée, salt and water. Bring to a boil, and simmer, uncovered, for 5 minutes. All the water should be absorbed. If not, continue to simmer until dry. Remove from the heat. Add the egg and raisins. Allow to cool completely.

Meanwhile, make the pastry. Cream together the butter and cream cheese. Sieve the flour and salt into a bowl, add to the creamed mixture, and mix well. Refrigerate for at least 1 hour.

Divide the pastry in half, and return half to the refrigerator. Divide the remaining dough into twelve equal balls. Roll out on a lightly floured surface into 7.5cm/3 inch circles. Fill with the cold meat mixture. Fold in half, and place on an ungreased baking sheet. Use the prongs of a fork to press the edges together. Continue until all the dough is used. Refrigerate the *empanadas* for at least 2 hours.

Bake in a moderate oven, 180°C/350°F/Gas 4, for 20 minutes, or until the *empanadas* are golden.

Variations

(1) Fill with a mixture of grated Wensleydale cheese and chopped green chillies.

(2) Fill with cooked chicken, grated Wensleydale cheese, chopped spring onion and chopped green chillies.

(3) A sweet variation is to fill each circle of dough with mincemeat. Sprinkle with caster sugar before baking.

Tostaditos de Queso
Toasted Cheese Snacks

Makes 18

18 × 7.5cm/3 inch Tortillas de Maíz *(page 14), cooked*
100g/4 oz Emmental cheese
Salsa Roja *(page 21)*
GARNISH:
2 jalapeño *peppers* or *Kenya chillies, sliced*

Spread the tortillas, evenly spaced, on a baking sheet. Layer on each a slice of cheese and a spoonful of *Salsa Roja*. Grill until the cheese has melted, approximately 3 minutes. Garnish with a thin slice of *jalapeño* pepper. Serve immediately.

Pepitas
Roasted Pumpkin Seeds

1 × 5ml spoon/1 teaspoon corn oil
100g/4 oz pumpkin seeds, unroasted
1 × 5ml spoon/1 teaspoon garlic salt
1 × 5ml spoon/1 teaspoon salt
a pinch of cayenne pepper
1–2 × 5ml spoons/1–2 teaspoons chilli powder

Heat the oil in a large frying pan. Add the pumpkin seeds, and move them around to prevent them from burning. Continue to cook until all the seeds are lightly browned.

Meanwhile, combine the garlic salt, salt, cayenne pepper and chilli powder in a small bowl.

When the pumpkin seeds are brown, drain them well on kitchen paper. While the seeds are still warm, put them in a bowl, pour the combined spices over, and stir until all the seeds are covered. Cool.

Store in an airtight container.

Note The seeds will keep crisp for up to 1 week.

A Selection of Cocktail Savouries
Layered Taco Dip (page 93), Nachos (page 88), Empanadas (page 89) and *Pepitas*

Botana de Frijoles
Bean Dip

Frijoles Refritos *(page 64)*
1–2 jalapeño *peppers* or *Kenya chillies, deseeded and chopped*
100g/4 oz Cheddar cheese, grated
a dash of Tabasco (optional)
spring onions with their tops, chopped

In a small flameproof casserole, combine the *Frijoles Refritos, jalapeño* peppers, 75g/3 oz of the cheese and the Tabasco, if using. Warm gently until the mixture is bubbling. Garnish with the spring onions and the remaining cheese. Serve on a hot plate, or over a candle, to keep the dip warm.

Serve with *Totopos* (page 16), corn chips or tortilla chips.

Botana de Picadillo y Queso
Chilli Cheese Dip

Picadillo *(page 17), made with 225g/8 oz minced beef*
150ml/¼ pint Salsa Picante *(page 22)*
450g/1 lb Cheddar cheese, grated

Heat the *Picadillo* in a pan with the *Salsa Picante*. Process in a food processor until smooth, or mash until as smooth as possible. Return the mixture to the pan, and heat. Add the cheese in four stages. Allow the cheese to melt completely before the next addition. Serve in a flameproof dish, kept warm on a hot plate or over a candle.

Serve with *Totopos* (page 16) or tortilla chips.

Note This is an excellent way to use up left-over *Picadillo*.

Botana de Tacos
Layered Taco Dip

Serves 12

Frijoles Refritos *(page 64)*
3 avocado pears
25ml/1 fl oz fresh lime juice
1 × 2.5ml spoon/½ teaspoon salt
300ml/½ pint soured cream
1–3 × 5ml spoons/1–3 teaspooons chilli powder
2 green chillies, finely chopped
1 × 5ml spoon/1 teaspoon ground cumin
1 bunch spring onions, chopped
3 tomatoes, skinned and chopped

Spread the *Frijoles Refritos* in a 25cm/10 inch pie plate.
Mash the avocado pears with the lime juice and salt, and spread on top of the beans.
Mix the soured cream with the chilli powder, chillies and cumin, and spread on top of the mashed avocado pears.
Mix the spring onions and tomatoes, and spread on top of the soured cream.
Continue to layer the ingredients in the order given, ending with a layer of spring onions and tomatoes.
Serve with *Totopos* (page 16) or tortilla chips.

Botana de Tamales
Tamale Dip

½ × 15ml spoon/½ tablespoon corn oil
1 medium onion, finely chopped
8 Tamales *(page 18), chopped*
300ml/½ pint Picadillo *(page 17)*
225g/8 oz Cheddar cheese, grated

Heat the oil in a medium flameproof casserole. Cook the onion until golden. Add the chopped *Tamales, Picadillo* and cheese. Heat the mixture over a medium heat, stirring all the time, until it is hot and the cheese is melted. Serve with *Totopos* (page 16).

Note This dip will use up left-overs. Increase or decrease the quantities, according to the amount of leftovers.

MENUS

The miscellany of flavours, aromas and textures in Mexican food can, at first, make putting together a meal seem a daunting task. The menus in this chapter will give you some ideas to start with, and you will soon find that devising your own combinations is easy, and fun. Remember, too, that many Mexican dishes go well with foods from other cuisines. Try *Ensalada de Nochebuena* (page 66) with a lamb chop, *Mole Poblano con Pollo* (page 45) with roast potatoes, or *Mousse de Rompope* (page 73) after poached salmon.

In Mexico, lunch is the main meal of the day. A 'typical' menu would start with a *sopa aguada* (wet soup), followed by a *sopa seca* (dry soup). Meat will come next, with a vegetable or salad, then beans and finally a sweet. Tortillas or bread and *salsas* (sauces) will be eaten with, and in between, courses.

As lunch is such a substantial meal, the other meals tend to be light. The day starts with coffee and *pan dulce* (sweet bread), and perhaps freshly squeezed orange juice, and at mid-morning there is more coffee and more *pan dulce*. The final meal of the day is a late supper, which could be an egg dish such as *Huevos con Chorizo y Papas* (page 48).

To drink with meals, there is wine or beer. Lager makes a good substitute for Mexican beer. Mexico also makes its own wines, although these are rarely exported. Instead, try the Spanish Riojas, both white and red.

Brunch for 12

Jugs of Lime Sangria Float (page 82)

•

Ranch-style Eggs (page 49)
Layered Taco Dip (page 93)
Black Beans (page 64)

•

Buñuelos (page 76)
Sopapillas (page 77)

•

Coffee Flavoured Crème Caramel (page 72)

•

Mexican Coffee (page 85)
Eggnog (page 86)

Dinner Party for Four

Guacamole (page 20) with Totopos (page 16)

•

Cebiche (page 54)

•

Puebla-style Chicken (page 45)
Mexican Rice (page 68)
Basic Beans (page 17)

•

Cauliflower Salad (page 65)

•

Eggnog Mousse (page 73)
Lime Sorbet (page 74)

•

Mexican Coffee (page 85)
Kahlúa Coffee (page 85)

INDEX